VICTORIAN
KITCHENS & BATHS

VICTORIAN
KITCHENS & BATHS

Franklin & Esther Schmidt

Gibbs Smith, Publisher
Salt Lake City

This book, as all our work, is dedicated to our eternally supportive parents, Joseph and Emma Schmidt, and Bernard and Marion Godwin, with love; also to Aunt Sid Goodman and Sim Franco, our caring, wise, funny and iconoclastic supra peers. Jigmop at Dogpatch is always at the heart of things.

First Edition

09 08 07 06 05   5 4 3 2 1

Text and photographs © 2005 Franklin & Esther Schmidt,

F & E Schmidt Photography, LLC

Published by

Gibbs Smith, Publisher

P.O. Box 667

Layton, Utah 84041

Orders: 1.800.748.5439

www.gibbs-smith.com

Designed by Tom Sieu and Dirk Walter

Endsheet wallpaper design courtesy of Bradbury & Bradbury Art Wallpapers

Printed and bound in Hong Kong

Library of Congress Cataloging-in-Publication Data

Schmidt, Franklin.

Victorian kitchens & baths / Franklin and Esther Schmidt.— 1st ed.

     p. cm.

ISBN 1-58685-302-3

1. Kitchens. 2. Bathrooms. 3. Interior decoration. 4. Decoration and ornament, Victorian style. I. Schmidt, Esther. II. Title.

NK2117.K5S364 2005

747.7'97—dc22

          2004021521

FOREWORD

I always thought it sensible that Victorians wallpapered their parlors and painted their kitchens and bathrooms, and strange that today we paint our living rooms and wallpaper our bathrooms and kitchens. But the history of the American kitchen and bath has been one of constant social, technological and psychological change. Walk into a twenty-first-century suburban house and the floor plan alone tells the story: the ample parlors and elaborate dining rooms of the nineteenth century are now merely vestigial. The once-simple kitchen has expanded to become the center of the house—a place for cooking, eating and informal family living. Similarly, the utilitarian Victorian bathroom has been superceded by dressing room/bathroom/spa combinations that would put an ancient Roman at ease. Why the changes?

In the nineteenth century, the kitchen was essentially a workroom—the domain of women, children and servants. But it was not always the romantic one of our imaginations. Before our era of neatly packaged and sanitized foods, blood and carcasses would have been a natural daily occurrence. The constant use of cast-iron stoves for baking the daily necessities made the kitchen unbearably hot during the summer months, so much so that "summer kitchens" were in common use around the country, ranging from elaborately equipped second kitchens away from the main living areas of the house, to the simple cast-iron stove on a porch. And, as it was not uncommon for a middle-class family to have a servant before World War I, class distinctions and racial prejudices also would have precluded the mixing of family and servants that a combination cooking/eating/social area would require.

The eat-in kitchen was popularized at the beginning of the twentieth century in the simple, space-conscious bungalow, and was made practical by the introduction of insulated gas and electric stoves. As cooking and food-preparation technologies continually advanced, the kitchen became larger and accommodated more family functions. And as the size and social importance of kitchens increased, the furniture and fittings that once would have only been seen in formal parlors and dining rooms found a new home in the family room. In our era, no expense is spared in making the kitchen both a beautiful and welcoming social space—call it the "parlorization" of the American kitchen.

As for bathrooms, the introduction of indoor plumbing in the nineteenth century was seen not only as a convenience, but also as a giant step forward in public health. The increasingly health-conscious Victorians saw their bathrooms as utilitarian bastions against the waves of contagious diseases such as cholera and typhoid that constantly threatened family health. As a result, the fitting of bathrooms was heavily influenced by the most sanitary of all institutions—the "modern" Victorian hospital. They were designed strictly for function; they were white, tiled, enameled and easy to clean. Today's carpeted and wallpapered bathrooms would have seemed unhealthy, unwise and, frankly, unsettling to an educated Victorian householder.

Today's romantically styled Victorian family rooms/kitchens and the elaborate bathrooms/spas present an exciting twenty-first-century evolution of nineteenth-century design. The challenge to the contemporary Victorian homeowner is a fascinating one: how to apply the principles of Victorian decorative design to rooms that were once considered merely functional. Nothing can be of greater help and pleasure than a splendidly photographed guidebook such as *Victorian Kitchens & Baths* that permits us to peer into the houses of fellow Victorian enthusiasts around the country, and to discover the exciting and innovative world that melds nineteenth-century aesthetics and twenty-first-century lifestyles.

—Bruce Bradbury
President and Founder
Bradbury & Bradbury Art Wallpapers

ACKNOWLEDGMENTS

To paraphrase the Beatles, in putting this book together "we got by with *a lot* of help from our friends."

We're most fortunate to be able to count as friends people for whom we've worked for years. They are also our editors and mentors. Each of them heads up one of the most respected and widely read magazines dealing with Victoriana—Patricia Poore, editor of *Old House Interiors* and Erika Kotite, editor of *Victorian Homes* magazine. Not only have they supported and encouraged our photography and writing, but they also generously contributed to this book their own well-written thoughts and expertise based on impressive experience and knowledge. We can't thank them enough.

We wish to acknowledge Bruce Bradbury's unique insights into the historic and contemporary Victorian worlds. His elegant vision keeps Victoriana shining.

Then, of course, is a group of perhaps some of the best minds and hands-on abilities in Victorian design, décor and construction. These people not only enriched this book with their contributions, but also have taught us much that we needed to know.

John Jowers of AntiqueAppliances.com stands out as a contributor who just about adopted this project as his own. Dan Mattausch, who is not only an expert in period lighting, but also in all things Victorian, and his wife, Nancy, allowed us to photograph their perfectly period kitchen throughout a long day and well into the night.

We thank, and acknowledge for his contribution, Robert Esposito, who could be called the ex-officio mayor of Williamsport, Pennsylvania. Robert's decorating prowess, insight and kindness added immensely to this book as well as our own knowledge.

Victoria Imperioli has an extraordinary knowledge of interior design, matched only by her experience in construction and her ability with a hammer. Victoria has added a special dimension to this book as well as our lives.

Talking about construction, where would any book on historic interiors be without perspectives on millwork? Brent Hull of Hull Historical, Inc., came through for us in spades.

In the same vein, no book on Victorian interiors would be complete without a discussion of stained and leaded glass. We are indebted to Rich and Jacki Kaiser for their thoughtful essay.

David Malkin, a British gentleman of the old school, graciously delved into his extensive experience in the world of tile to educate us about its use during the Victorian period; thank you, David.

Special thanks are due to Catherine Sieberling Pond, who wrote an enlightening piece on Victorian pantries, and to Dudley Brown, the Grand Wizard of Victorian design.

All the homeowners, who not only graciously invited us to photograph their kitchens and baths and made it fun, but also took time out of their own professional and personal schedules to write their diaries, are owed a special note of gratitude. They went beyond hospitable and gracious; we value their friendship:

Jean Dunbar and Peter Sils, who were most generous hosts;
Our Yankee compatriot and kindred spirit, Ann Tobias;
Marcia Miele, who made us part of her community of friends and family;
Bruce Johnson, who influenced our perceptions of how artful one can be in re-creating a Victorian sensibility.

We'd like to thank the good people at Thomas Crapper, Ltd., who came through for us, meeting an unreasonable deadline with goodwill.

Sheila Parkert, owner and designer of the most elegant Victorian hotel we've ever seen, the Adelphi in Saratoga Springs, New York, is an encouraging supporter and friend. We thank her for introducing us to Zachary Solov, who, despite his celebrity, treated us mere mortals with patient respect.

We are most grateful to Florine McCain, editor of *Victorian Decorating,* published by Harris Publications, for her years-long friendship and professional guidance.

Marilyn Hansen, our first editor, is owed a big thank-you for her encouragement in our early years in this business.

So many people throughout the country were incredibly kind in welcoming us into their homes; the list and appropriate acknowledgments would equal the size of this book. However, we would like to acknowledge a representative handful who stand out in our memories. This is not to ignore so many others who were equally kind and hospitable.

Thank you:

Mary Ann and Norman Davidson of Independence, Missouri, who made their mansion and home our home; the Barrois family—by way of the most talented Jeff Gueno—of Lafayette, Louisiana; the Miller clan formerly of Peru, Indiana, who welcomes us every time we came through with our cameras; the Cardens in Kinsale, Virginia; all the wonderful historic preservationists in the Quapaw District of Little Rock, Arkansas. Henry and Mary Collings, who introduced us to their community of Williamsport, Pennsylvania, a mecca of Victoriana—and all the gracious people there whose homes we photographed; the exciting Victorian historians of San Francisco, California; the most knowledgeable curators of the Laura Ingalls Wilder homestead in DeSmet, South Dakota; Laura Bachelor, executive director of the unique Swiss Tinker Cottage Museum in Rockford, Illinois; the great staff at the Riordan Mansion in Flagstaff, Arizona; the folks at the National Park Service for letting us in "where no man has tread before"; the staff of the mayor's office in New Orleans, Louisiana, who just about stand on their heads to make our work go smoothly; Peter Yokum (artist extraordinaire) and Polly Anderson, who make this business fun.

Special thanks to "favorite Auntie Tanya" and all her beautiful kids for being our friends.

We appreciate Lynn Moriarity for helping us stay organized and on target; we know it isn't easy. We're grateful to M. J. Stiers for her support and friendship. As always, photography master Isaac Abramson continues to influence.

Luba and Pincus, you're always with us.

We're especially grateful to our editor, Aimee Stoddard, whose professional and exhaustive effort made this book what we always wanted it to be.

Thank you, Michael and Carmen, for being stalwart supporters.

We always want to acknowledge the remarkable, irreplaceable Godwin clan—Dito, Beth, Bernie and August—our loyal defenders, best buddies and closest allies.

—*Franklin & Esther Schmidt*

INTRODUCTION

Romance is in—again—which is probably why Victorian design and architecture are as popular now as they were from the middle of the nineteenth century to the beginning of the twentieth century when Victorian was the contemporary style. The essence of Victorian design lies in its warm woods, opulence, colors and patterns. But beyond the look, our continuing draw to it is based on ties to family histories and memories of past generations. Houses with turrets, gingerbread and multiple porches are being bought or built by people with a passion for preservation, an eye for romantic high style and a love of the pieces of the past we can make our own. It's a contagious enthusiasm that doesn't dissipate.

Those who buy or build Victorian often have expertise in antiques of the era and can knowledgeably furnish a period living room or bedroom, but when it comes to doing the kitchen or bathroom, they are stymied. There are also those who are not necessarily aficionados of Victorian high style, but are drawn to certain elements that they would like to translate into their more contemporary homes, particularly in their kitchens and bathrooms.

Mid-nineteenth and early-twentieth-century kitchens were almost solely utilitarian workrooms, the denizen of the servants and not of the family. Today's kitchen has evolved into a social center where work, leisure and entertainment combine to create an environment that needs to be attractive as well as functional. Islands, eating nooks, window treatments, artwork and investment in the most attractive and up-to-date appliances (or the most effective way of disguising them) can make the kitchen the greatest financial investment in a house.

(left) *This stylish new Victorian bathroom is the epitome of romantic. The mood, rather than specific design elements, makes it Victorian.*

(right) *There were just a few simple elements in this late-nineteenth-century midwestern kitchen. An open cupboard for dishware, a wood cook stove and a hearth helped to provide three meals a day for a large family.*

(above) *Designer Dudley Brown created a new Victorian kitchen and family area by bor-rowing elements from the exterior design and architecture of this circa-1900 house near the Potomac River in southeastern Virginia. The etched-glass design in the door at left is borrowed from the design of the house's original weathervane. In the family room, the low-set mullion in the window follows the height of the exterior veranda. Trims are dis-tinctly Victorian and the upholstered furniture suggests the soft lines of the period.*

(opposite page, left) *This more formal Victorian-style break-fast nook was added adjacent to, but not as part of, the Victorian kitchen in this period house in Williamsport, Pennsylvania.*

(opposite page, right) *This eat-in area was installed in the kitchen of a Gothic Carpenter cottage in Maine.*

Except in the most traditional household or the purest Victorian-period home, the dining room is becoming a space of the past—in use for company but not for family meals. Breakfast nooks, either part of the kitchen or adjacent to it, are now automatic inclusions in new homes or old-house remodels and serve as the three-meal dining area.

Today's bathroom also follows this cultural transformation in design, décor and function. Originally an unadorned room that, after the Industrial Revolution, occasionally incorporated elaborately designed fixtures, the bathroom was most often décor devoid. Bathroom innovations were more about function than form. High tech to those in the mid- to late nineteenth century, innovative bathroom appliances were usually more about improvements in personal hygiene than design chic.

During the past half century, the world of bathrooms has changed in staggering proportions. While guest bathrooms might still be fairly modest in size and facilities, master baths have taken off into a world of their own. Newly constructed and refurbished bathrooms are often larger than most newlyweds' first apartments. Multiple sinks and showerheads; saunas; two-person tubs; elaborate, decorative tiles; and lighting fixtures are the norm. The bathroom is now a room of myriad creature comforts—a virtual vacation spot at home. To this, we add Victorian style for a twenty-first-century amalgam of old-world charm and modern comfort.

In *Victorian Kitchens & Baths,* we deconstruct both the historic and contemporary Victorian-style kitchen and bathroom. We look at the individual design, décor and architectural elements that make these rooms Victorian. We do this through photographs taken of a huge range of

Victorian designs and explain in caption and text those elements that have come together to create the entire look. We and experts in their respective fields offer views of Victorian design and specific tips on just how to arrive at the extraordinary finished product.

We've discovered, after years of writing about and photographing the world of Victoriana, that—to borrow an expression—you can put two people in a Victorian room and you'd get three opinions on what the room's all about. It's a matter of subjective and individual perception. There are absolutists who proclaim that all Victorians would do something this way or that. One editor insisted that "all Victorians were neat and even their clutter was well organized." All Victorians? There's no such thing as "all Victorians." Given that there really are no rules, one can't say that there are hard-and-fast specific timelines when one Victorian look or style began and another ended in all places, with all people—and that all Victorian homeowners did everything inside and outside their homes exactly according to any particular style.

Style and décor, then as now, were open to personal comfort and interpretation. It is not revisionist to suggest that Victorian was a sensibility more than a definitive system of decorative and architectural values. Those values did exist, but more as general parameters and guidelines than as rigid disciplines, despite what one might read by self-proclaimed icons, past and present.

For example, we can say that as a general rule, in that era, tin ceilings had application in commercial buildings such as stores and saloons and were not used in private residences. However, we can't say that no Victorian would have put a tin ceiling in a kitchen. And, while there are purists who object vehemently to the concept, if someone wants to put a tin ceiling in a Victorian-style kitchen today, no design rule says it shouldn't be done.

Conversely, there were definite design influences that can be seen throughout Victorian décor, such as a focus on nature and natural building elements and a fascination for exotic travel. These were parlayed into a variety of Victorian decorating elements that we see over a sixty-year period reflected in countless expressions.

So, purists beware. We believe and hope you'll find information in these pages that are true to form in historic Victorian style according to historians, museum house directors, curators and other purists. However,

(above) *Victorian design elements are incorporated into this Lafayette, Louisiana, bathroom.*

you'll also see interpretive style and design that are favored by the many who love the period but take only those parts that suit them best. We offer what we think is the best of both worlds, which is really one very large world of Victoriana.

We look at historic Victorian kitchens as they existed or have been researched and then reconstructed in museum houses. We examine and analyze kitchens in both historic and new houses that have borrowed some specifically traditional Victorian design elements from the era, and we

These homeowners added a sauna while maintaining a distinctly Victorian décor in this bathroom. It clearly shows how one can stay in period and have all the luxuries of the twenty-first century without breaking a sweat.

✳ ✳ ✳ ✳ ✳

define how and why they work. In doing this, we point out and explain Victorian-specific elements of design and architecture as they were applied during that period, or have been applied later to make a design statement.

Both product experts as well as Victorian publishing personalities offer their unique perspectives, tips and ideas about Victorian kitchens and bathrooms. Among those who contribute their ideas and expertise are Erika Kotite, board member of the Victorian Society in America and editor of *Victorian Homes* magazine, and Patricia Poore, editor of *Old House Interiors*.

Throughout the text of this book, one may find some redundancies and even some contradictions. Our contributing writers do not always share the same views and opinions. However, we feel that it is essential to include the substance of their observations. We also believe that some seemingly overlapping information is well worth restating within the context of these experts' visions. Doing this, we believe, brings the book full circle within a range of highly individual perspectives.

Victorian Kitchens & Baths, in addition to devoting attention to new and refurbished Victorian kitchens and bathrooms, goes on to a fanciful and creative take on Victorian as designed by people who love the idea of this style and added some innovative strokes of their own. Given that, all kitchens serve the same function and all baths are still a home's necessity. It's how people have actualized their creative instincts or manifested their desire for restoration and preservation of golden times past that have given grist to our photographic and editorial mill.

We're constantly amazed and impressed by the creativity, vision and talent expressed by homeowners in designing and redesigning their kitchens and bathrooms. Each household has the unique design imprint of its owner; each, to some degree, is an interpretation of the homeowner's vision of, and affection for, Victorian style. Some focus on emphasizing woodwork and cabinetry while others emphasize color, texture and pattern or dazzling stained glass and lighting fixtures.

We are also awed by the number of people who rescue historic houses—hands on. There are people in their twenties to those in their eighties who remove paint, scour floors, hang wallpaper and refinish their own homes inch by inch over months and years. Many of them could well afford to hire others to do the work but would never dream of anything but personal renovation. Home becomes hobby, friend, pet and passion.

We located houses of almost every style built in the Victorian period and some that are no more than one or two years old. Those in cities range from elaborate high-style Queen Anne to the less-embellished, linear house typical of the mission style popular toward the end of Victoriana. Some of the rural houses are simple Prairie-style farmhouses and a few have log kitchens.

When we were first assigned to photograph and write about a Victorian house many years ago, we felt like strangers in a strange land. Our innocence and ignorance left us bewildered as to what we were viewing—and more importantly—photographing. We really believed Eastlake was somewhere near Lake Superior and that an Arts and Crafts house was filled with jigsawed, wooden cutouts of teddy bears and quilts with appliqués.

Over time, we were introduced to the indelible art and craftsmanship of the great nineteenth- and early-twentieth-century design visionaries like Belter, Belcher and Stickley, and to a lifestyle still relished. So many people—historians, homeowners, editors, experts and passionate collectors—unraveled their mysterious and beautiful worlds of design and lifestyle. We began to see this lush and rich high style with new eyes.

We now move comfortably and happily in the world of Victoriana and continue to be amazed by the creative and artistic riches it offers. Every house we photograph, every Victorian street we pass, every passionate resident of a period home we meet gives us greater respect and appreciation for the era and those who live in its world.

This has been an exhilarating project. To encapsulate the extraordinarily diverse range of visions people have for their most important living spaces into one volume has, at once, been a challenge and a painful pleasure. There was so much from which we could glean.

This diverse group of kitchens and bathrooms, reflecting the largest possible variety of locale, income level and style of the Victorian sensibility, gives an expanded perception of the possibilities in our own homes.

Despite its lack of ornamentation, this historically pure Victorian kitchen offers elements that today's kitchen designers continue to emulate. Note open shelves with crockery, the table/island work area and white-painted trim for ease of cleaning. We may enrich these in color and texture, but the basics remain comforting and appealing.

Historic Victorian

✳ ✳

Setting the Stage

Most people define the Victorian period historically from 1837, the year of Queen Victoria's ascension to the throne, to 1901, the year of her death. The great Victorian design years in the United States run from the mid-1800s to the first few years of the twentieth century, and it is these years on which we focus text and images of this book. Houses built during that period were often large and ornate, especially those in major towns and cities. In the countryside and in farm country, architecture was far simpler and more informal.

In almost any house, especially in the earliest Victorian years, the kitchen was not included in the design or décor concepts of the rest of the house. Kitchens were just becoming attached and built onto the main house. In earlier house design (the Colonial and Federal periods), cooking facilities were often housed in a building separate from the main residence for safety reasons. Open-hearth cooking and therefore open fireplaces were dangerous. Accidental fires burned down many kitchen structures, so their placement detached from the main house prevented many tragedies.

Through the early to mid-Victorian era, kitchens in urban, middle-class households were often in the basement, generally dismal and mainly frequented by servants rather than homeowners. Standard kitchen design meant plaster or tile walls, an open hearth or wood- or coal-burning cook stove, a worktable and some shelving. Generally, it was austere and clean—as clean as the guidelines of sanitation during those times would suggest.

(above) *This kitchen at the Farmington House in Louisville, Kentucky, actually predates the Victorian era but offers almost the same design. In fact, little changed in kitchen design until the Industrial Revolution of the mid-nineteenth century eventually brought advanced appliances and new methods of refrigeration, cooking and food storage.*

(opposite page) *The large, open hearth is the center of this historic kitchen. The center table could have been used as a workstation but also probably served as a dining table for the servants. Note the kitchen on page 64 to see how a contemporary homeowner placed her stove in a like manner.*

As all things in design, there are no hard-and-fast rules. This exquisite room with its fresco paintings in the Tinker Swiss Cottage in Rockford, Illinois, is the exception to the accepted notion that most Victorian kitchens were unadorned.

The layout of the kitchen was not the designer's triangle of today—sink, stove and refrigerator, including easy access to the microwave and dishwasher. Food preparation started from scratch. It was not necessary for the cook to do a graceful pirouette in one 45-degree motion as she took an item from the icebox, rinsed it off, seasoned it and popped it in the oven. There were no thirty-minute freezer-to-table masterpieces at that time.

The middle-class Victorian kitchen was, in understatement, a constant rolling thunder of activity. In the morning, the family, unlike Ozzie and Harriet or the Osbournes, did not grab munchies or granola bars and run. Breakfast was a major meal prepared by kitchen staff who would often get up before daybreak to begin the day's efforts.

Gilbert and Sullivan, in their nineteenth-century operetta *The Sorcerer*, refer to the English breakfast—the American one wasn't much different:

> *Now to the banquet we press;*
> *Now for the eggs, the ham;*
> *Now for the mustard and cress;*
> *Now for the strawberry jam.*
> *Now for the tea of our host,*
> *Now for the rollicking bun;*
> *Now for the muffins and toast . . .*

That was just part of it; and that was just breakfast.

Entertaining one's friends was the heart of Victorian society. There was a spectacular array of silverware to be constantly cleaned—asparagus and oyster forks, grapefruit spoons and olive spears—and the meals were just as layered and complicated. One's position in society was often measured by the quality and elaboration involved in entertaining, and societal position was (as still is) everything.

Marilyn Hansen, former magazine editor and cookbook writer, in her 1990 volume *Entertaining in the Victorian Style,* describes how her grandmother, a cook for a Victorian family in the 1880s, would often say, "I would rather give a dinner party than have a new dress." Ms. Hansen goes on to describe how, when the master and mistress of the house would go away, Ms. Hansen's grandparents invited their own friends to the house, where they cooked and served an elaborate dinner in the manner to which they wished they were born.

COME THE REVOLUTION

In the last half of the nineteenth century, the world changed dramatically, courtesy of the Industrial Revolution. New technology inspired social and cultural changes at a then-unprecedented pace, forever altering the basics of American life. By the early twentieth century, there were hundreds of applications for patents on improved toilets. Factory-canned goods filled storage pantries previously containing only crocks and bins of flour and other staples. At the time when people were overwhelmed by such marvels as the telephone and boxed cereals, hundreds of small kitchen appliances, gadgets and tools were being patented and were filling Victorian kitchens.

Consistent with all these technological and scientific changes—dizzying even to the most progressive Victorian mind—industry increasingly hired women as workers who, until then, could only find employment as domestics. Factories and offices offered opportunities in pay and freedom that were, until then, unavailable. Previously, domestic servants would often even take board as part of their employment condition. Now, with other opportunities attracting women, they suddenly had the freedom to live on their own, without the necessity of being under their employers' roofs 24/7. Middle-class families couldn't compete. Even though in 1900 the average wage in the United States was less than 25 cents an hour and fewer than 10 percent of Americans graduated from high school, everybody strove to climb a rung.

Social intercourse, culture, industry and technological innovation all were interdependent factors affecting society and, eventually, the lifestyle within a household.

Then, except for the upper classes who didn't have to struggle to meet the higher wage demands of employees, the family began incorporating the kitchen as an integral part of the home, not merely as a workstation to be utilized by their help.

Historical perception has a way of telescoping events, taking that which occurs over time and summarizing it as though change occurred overnight. Also, in our contemporary society, we've become used to a quick-change lifestyle via computers, cell phones and other innovations that almost instantly alter our way of doing things. This, of course, was not the case in the nineteenth century. Lifestyle patterns were slow to change, evolving over years and even decades.

While canned pork and beans and soups became available in the 1860s, it wasn't until the 1880s that evaporated milk was sold. Saccharin and milk chocolate were produced in 1879, with Dr. Pepper and Coca-Cola stocking shelves a year later. It was at least a decade later before someone thought of selling Cracker Jacks and going out to a local pizza parlor.

It wasn't until the turn of the century that some Victorian whiz kids dreamt up tea bags and instant coffee. A can and a jar at a time, kitchen life changed.

As domestic servants became less easily accessible and more costly, and household chores changed from being exhausting and never ending to tediously overwhelming, housewives and mothers found themselves taking on some of the chores.

Even into the early twentieth century, the domestic as part of the family structure was more the rule. Consider what an *Encyclopedia Britannica* published in the early 1920s had to say about it:

> ### HOUSEKEEPING IN THE SERVANTLESS HOME
>
> Owing to the scarcity and relative inefficiency of domestics combined with the increased cost of living and wages, a very large number of housewives who previously kept one or two maids now prefer to do their own work, and provided the members of the family appreciate the changed conditions, the running of a servantless house need not deprive the housewife of her outside interests, friends and pleasures.

While the cheery face of the all-American Campbell's Soup kid

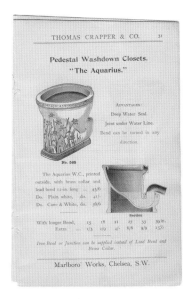

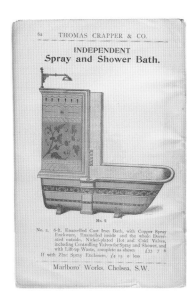

peered at our ancestors from can labels in the kitchen, the urban, middle-class American housewife learned to make do with one house servant at a time—and even that period was soon to come to a close.

The bathroom, too, saw some changes. It has been said that the difference between a poor family and a rich one in early to mid-Victorian times was that the rich had people to empty their chamber pots for them. Eventually, people didn't need that service at all. In the 1860s carpenters in the cities and homeowners in the country followed plans to build one-seat privies with mechanical contrivances designed to close the hopper after deposits were made. A short twenty years later, people began flushing with regularity.

AMERICA FIRST

The changes brought into the home from the 1860s to the turn of the century encompassed a steady stream of new ideas, not the least of which was America's realization that it needed to be taken seriously, on its own terms, in style and design. Invention, technical advances and modernizations were one thing; the aesthetics of a nation that was entering the world community was another dimension entirely.

While the middle and upper classes traversed the globe and brought back exotica with which to style their interiors, they also wanted to show the world that we were a nation who enjoyed its own artistic creations. America was to proudly jut out its technological and economic might to the rest of civilization. Surely we could also brave a new world of culture—we were tired of taking a backseat to old-world art, design and décor.

Materialism through the acquisition of stuff was a new standard of interior design, and Victorians were the epitome of eclectic collectors. This attitude created a design sensibility during those years of Victoria's reign that has imprinted our society through the present.

We were anglophiles; we based our home fashions on a British queen. But, being Americans, we still needed to outdo our mentors, out-Victorianize Victoria. Now we had the wherewithal to do it.

Manufacturing, modified tools, and creative and expert immigrant craftsmen, who could be hired for little more than what it cost to feed them, all contributed to the gilding, painting and filigreeing of America's towns and cityscapes. No line was left uncurved, no room left unpainted or wall unpapered. Painted ladies dominated Main Streets, and barbers everywhere were beleaguered to furnish cut hair for plasterers to include in their interior corbels. Victoriana was the rage that raged on.

Then came the bathroom—Americanized. While Thomas Crapper was creating bathroom fixtures for the nobility and ladies and gentlemen of the British realm, and establishing a name that after World War I would be recognized (albeit demeaningly) throughout the world, J. L. Mott's Iron Works produced a catalog in 1888 offering Americans, who also needed to go to the bathroom, hundreds of choices in fixtures, fittings, designs and details. Typical of American excess of the period, Mott's toilets used as many as ten gallons of water per flush.

The times, they were a-changing. As America and the world approached the last century of the previous millennium, inventions, modernizations and style changes came to be expected. We looked forward to the future. In all but the most rural communities, bathrooms were standard accessories and kitchens began expanding to incorporate breakfast areas where families would actually sit within view of the work areas. As happens with any fashion, it was time to look down a different road.

WE WERE CRAFTY

As chauvinistic as we were, once again, however, America followed the lead of the British; we couldn't help it. We reacted with simpatico to William Morris and others who dealt with the industrial excesses of a new-world order and recoiled from the elaboration of Victoriana. They created the vision for a style where man employed his artistry and craftsmanship in everyday life.

According to the deftly written *Rejuvenation Catalog:*

> The Arts and Crafts movement originated in mid-nineteenth-century England with social reformers John Ruskin and William Morris. They believed that the only success the Industrial Revolution could claim—with its smoke-belching factories full of dehumanized and impoverished workers—was the mass-production of ugliness and unhappiness. Their solution? A return to work with heart. Inspired by an idealized vision of medieval craft guilds and the dignity of handwork, these men championed a new form of industry, where things of beauty made with pride by artisans and craftsmen, brought pleasure to the user and the maker. This basic idea quickly blossomed into the Arts and

Crafts movement, an international trend that influenced architecture and the decorative arts well into the twentieth century.

> In America, where industrialization had been less destructive, the Arts and Crafts movement was given a different twist. Lacking a medieval craft tradition, being closer to nature, and feeling less ambivalent about the benefits of technology, Arts and Crafts proponents like Elbert Hubbard and Gustav Stickley mixed manpower, machine power, marketing power and the power of Mother Nature in a unique recipe intended to make a rich life available to all. . . . Out was the bric-a-brac of the materialistic Gilded Age mansion.

The kitchen and bathroom were—and are—slow to follow new design trends and remodels. But follow they did, and eventually these rooms took the giant step into stylistic integration with the rest of the house.

Then, in the early 1920s, the Arts and Crafts period ebbed and we began our first baby steps into the modern era.

WHAT COMES AROUND GOES AROUND

Today, we've come full circle. We are ready to look at our kitchens and baths and, as homeowners did a century ago, incorporate the architectural and design elements that make them livable spaces. We love what we perceive as the more elegant gilded age, or the quieter Arts and Crafts period. We want to return—if, not exactly as it was—to how we would like it to have been.

Having said all of the above, one thing is always true. There are exceptions to everything. There may have been some free-spirited Victorian souls who could no more pass up a chance to make the kitchen a more artfully designed space. There are people in the twenty-first century who share the Victorians' plain design aesthetic when it comes to kitchen décor. We have seen fully plumed Victorian houses decorated in a twenty-first-century rendition of historic Victorian style. When it came to the kitchen, those homeowners have preferred to maintain the simple and stark look that was true to the historic Victorian kitchen. This applies to bathrooms, as well. So, while the accessories and appliances are up-to-date,

the look is as simple as it was 125 years ago. Today, in many ways, we're looking forward to the past. As every politician knows, history is what you interpret it to be.

HISTORIC PURITY IN TWENTY-FIRST-CENTURY LIFE

For those with a grand passion for the history and design of the Victorian era, there is no way to go when designing a kitchen or bathroom except to stay true to the period. The following kitchen journals record how two different homeowners transformed their original nineteenth-century cooking spaces into modern, functioning kitchens while painstakingly trying to retain every bit of their original architecture and design.

They each scrupulously researched the history of their houses and adopted design details such as cabinet style and material from other rooms, repeating them in the kitchen. They were both exacting in their approach, tireless in their quest for uncovering original architectural elements and did a great deal of the actual construction work themselves. The result, in both cases, are kitchens that look as much like one would imagine they would have at the time the houses were new, had the modern conveniences we now take for granted been available at that time.

There are major differences between the two: in the Mattausch kitchen, there are almost no visible traces of contemporary kitchen conveniences, while in the Sils Dunbar kitchen, there has been only a minimal attempt to disguise most of the contemporary functioning parts of their kitchen. They have instead incorporated them into the old-world design typical of the rest of their house.

In a sense, there is a progression from one to the other, the Mattausch project being as historically pure as possible, the Sils Dunbar project allowing for the new but putting it in the context of old. Despite their different approaches, what they both share is not only an actualization of unrelenting effort, but an elegance that reflects the epitome of period Victoriana.

(above) *The wallpaper in this period-Victorian house is certainly as lovely as any that would have been found in the more public rooms of this grand house.*

(right) *Period simplicity is the key to the design of this bathroom with its wainscoting, simple shelf and mirror, and shuttered windows.*

(opposite) *Located in the Wellscroft Lodge near Lake Placid, New York, this grand Arts and Crafts bathroom is at once up to the times technologically as well as stylistically integrated into the design of the rest of the house. The tile work on the floor and the curtained shower are typical of the period.*

A VICTORIAN KITCHEN DIARY

By Dan and Nancy Mattausch

When restoring a period home, one of the first questions to come up is, "What to do with the kitchen?" Technological advances came fast and furious in the nineteenth century and Victorians were quick to adopt the most advanced gadgets to be had. Thus, the spirit of the age would allow for the most modern kitchen currently available. This presents a major problem in terms of design, however, as stainless steel and chrome do not mix well with heart pine and soapstone. Our solution was to have the best of both worlds: a technologically advanced kitchen with the uncompromised appearance of the Victorian heart of the home. As you can see in the photographs, our kitchen certainly looks like a house museum, complete with working electric-start gaslights. What you cannot see (although they are in the photographs) are the Traulsen commercial refrigerator/freezer and ice maker, the two Fisher & Paykel dishwashers, the Viking trash compactor, the Míele convection steam oven, the microwave, the toaster oven and the Internet, TV/DVD, high-speed communications center.

All it takes is time, money, creativity and a certain wild-eyed fanaticism that ignores the pleas of the kitchen-cabinet salesman at the home improvement store. When planning for this kitchen, our first task was to determine how the room was originally laid out. While we like to think of ourselves as so modern and advanced (compared to those quaint Victorians), our experience has been that nineteenth-century homes are usually very well thought out *if you understand them.* Instead of trying to impose modern fashion on a home that has stood the test of time, the house will often work much better if used as it was intended.

Our home had been abused as an art gallery and an office before we purchased it, so our first thought was that the kitchen was a blank canvas. Upon closer inspection, however, we realized that all the original built-in kitchen cabinets were intact (albeit buried under nearly twenty layers of paint), the brickwork for the coal stove was present (under the same paint),

The Mattausch kitchen is in the home of a former staff member of President Theodore Roosevelt. While utilizing it as full-time kitchen today, the owners believe this room looks just about like it did during Roosevelt's tenure. It's one of the few truly historic kitchens that is still functional.

(top right) *The antique-style cabinet doors on the left open to twenty-first-century refrigeration units. The handcrafted woodwork is period appropriate.*

(bottom right) *The original built-in cabinets not only hold the collectible jars, cans and boxes, most of which originate from the late nineteenth century to the early part of the twentieth century, but also function as pantry cabinet space for today's everyday food-prep supplies.*

(left) *This Centennial sink backsplash is a Victorian treasure hunter's dream; it is rare to find one, let alone in mint condition. The Mattausches were beside themselves when they discovered it.*

Dan and Nancy's water heater is original to the kitchen; the stove is a contemporary appliance manufactured in the Victorian style. The view is into the pantry area.

Note the wainscoting and the receipt hook on the wall behind the table. Very few people are fortunate enough to find a historic house with so many of its original architectural elements in good condition. The number of people who can then refurbish it to authentic period style is far less. This was one lucky house to find owners such as Dan and Nancy, who not only love the house, but also were able to refurbish and restore it to its historic purity.

and holes in the wainscot indicated precisely where the kitchen sink had been. All that was needed was the icebox, stove and the center table before the kitchen could come back to life.

One of the most difficult design decisions when creating a modern Victorian kitchen is how to conceal a refrigerator, which is a contemporary device that has fairly uniform dimensions. No matter what sort of panels you put on the doors, it still looks like a refrigerator. We chose a commercial refrigerator because of the unusual combination of two doors and three drawers. With the doors and a drawer sheathed in mahogany and the lower drawers in pine wainscot, the refrigerator began to assume the shape of a traditional built-in icebox instead of an electric refrigerator. By venting the refrigerator through the top, we were able to cover the front louvers, and with the addition of period hinges, latches and a label, the transformation was complete.

The rarest item in the kitchen is unquestionably the cast-iron backsplash on the sink. While white enameled sinks (from the early twentieth century) can regularly be located in salvage yards, we have yet to see an intact nineteenth-century cast-iron kitchen sink outside of a house museum. We purchased the backsplash many years ago in Brimfield, Massachusetts, to rescue it as an orphan piece long separated from its sink. When we discovered the current availability of soapstone sheets (which can be cut with carbide woodworking tools), we realized that this sink back could be used as a focal point. A modern mixer faucet and valve even allowed for the use of an old spigot.

We are very pleased with our "new" kitchen that fits in perfectly with the other historically furnished rooms in our home and functions as well as or better than the most contemporary-looking kitchen available. The total lack of modern kitchen cabinets is more than compensated for by the center table, which provides space equal to sixteen linear feet of countertop and the built-in cabinets that allow for a wall full of storage. We think the photographs show that sometimes you can bake your cake and eat it too.

Dan Mattausch is an internationally recognized expert on nineteenth-century lighting whose essay on that topic appears on page 89. He and his wife, Nancy, have restored a nineteenth-century Washington, D.C., house.

PRESTON STREET KITCHEN
By Jean Dunbar and Peter Sils

A previous owner had divided our 1892 Anglo-Japanese-style house into four apartments. In its first incarnation, it had been the spacious residence of its architect, William G. McDowell, but we lived in a small second-floor unit and rented out the rest.

During the house's years as an apartment building, the original kitchen—always without counters—had been remodeled into a bedroom and bathroom, and the butler's pantry had been fitted up as a tiny kitchen, of sorts. The space was so small that you could wear it. Once we returned the house to its single-family layout, we immediately undertook creating an efficient and spacious kitchen.

Our first priority was to make sure that this kitchen would blend with the house, while accommodating our passion for cooking. As usual, the Secretary of the Interior's Standards for Rehabilitation and Guidelines for Rehabilitating Historic Buildings guided the design. This document, which sets federal standards for work on old buildings, promotes preserving or restoring original spaces and proportions, and retaining original materials. So we kept the original configuration of the butler's pantry and kitchen, adding only a small closet.

A peninsula, clad in tongue-and-groove wainscot, salvaged from elsewhere in the room, and an under-counter oven helped increase counter space. We stripped latex paint from the original varnished woodwork, stained it with a mixture of two penetrating stains and sealed everything with waterproof spar varnish. The louver door on the new closet got the same treatment.

A new kitchen in an old house is always a fantasy since appliances and fitted cabinets had no place in nineteenth-century kitchens. Two possibilities always have merit: a kitchen that keeps the unfitted look of historic kitchens, concealing the new in the old and avoiding fitted cabinets; or a kitchen that takes its cues from the butler's pantry—a traditional home of storage and counters.

Given our limited budget and a house-wide dearth of storage, the butler's pantry strategy won out—especially since Euro-style cabinets with flush doors could conceal inexpensive melamine-coated cabinet boxes that were made and installed by a local cabinet shop. We chose a manufactured, unfinished cherry door with striations that echoed those of the

(opposite page, top) *The dining-breakfast nook, just off the kitchen workspace, is conveniently twentieth century, and its millwork and ambiance matches perfectly with the antique sense of the kitchen.*

(opposite page, bottom) *The hardware in Jean and Peter's kitchen was of their own creative effort. They bought the pulls and standards separately and combined them for effect. It works. The refrigerator is just to the left.*

(above) *The Dunbar-Sils kitchen has the spacious appeal and workability most homeowners desire. And, as Jean describes it, she has the best of both worlds—a new kitchen in an old house.*

(right) *This corner molding is repeated throughout the house—in the kitchen doorways and the bathrooms. It is this kind of detailed workmanship that cries out to design- and history-savvy people to buy and restore historic structures.*

house's trim. Reproduction brass back plates combined with black wooden knobs strengthened the Anglo-Japanese look. Glass-fronted upper cabinets, built of high-quality plywood, received the same penetrating stain used elsewhere.

Much of the look of the kitchen comes from its soapstone counters. The material was used for both counters and sinks in the nineteenth century. Once rubbed with linseed oil, soapstone is impervious to heat and spills. Here, an extra-deep stainless steel under-mounted sink—fabricated by a restaurant supplier—substitutes convincingly for a historically accurate zinc one. A convenient drain board is carved into the soft stone.

The floor in the second-floor conservatory suggested the 1 x 1–inch mosaic tiles. American Olean set up the colors and pattern we selected in 1 x 2–foot sheets for ease of installation. The walls' grayish green—much loved by the Aesthetic movement that influenced the house—was the original color in the house's first-floor bedroom and bath. The Bradbury & Bradbury Penelope Border adds contrast and aesthetic detail.

To ensure adequate light, we combined unobtrusive "eyeball" lights directed at work areas with reproduction pendant lights by St. Louis Antique Lighting over the counters and table. Halophane shades allow maximum illumination—important in a room partly shaded by a porch. A light in the venting hood shines directly on the Thermador cooktop. Like the earliest iceboxes, the Sub-Zero refrigerator is clad in wood paneling. A mirror, a German extension table and circa-1890 to 1910 Thonet bentwood chairs add to the furnished feel of the room. Unlike Victorian kitchens, this one provides a setting for parties as well as canning marathons.

Given the chance to revisit the design process with a bigger budget, we would make just a few changes. We'd sacrifice a few inches of counter to allow for a slightly larger refrigerator. The noisy fan in the stove hood would be moved to a remote location. And the cabinets—traditional "carcass" style, rather than cost-effective, but more modern Euro style—would reach to the ceiling to provide even more storage. Then, again, we'd hate to change a kitchen that many visitors believe to be original!

(left) *Simple and austere, the incredible woodwork is wonderful. Not all bathrooms need to be Taj Mahals.*

(opposite) *The shutters in this room open vertically, which is a most unusual and very appealing configuration.*

ORIGINAL BATHROOM

The shape of the house's original bathroom has been changed slightly to accommodate a sauna and shower. Wainscot matched to the room's original wainscot camouflages these additions. The American Olean mosaic floor uses colors available in the 1890s, when the house was built; tiling extends into the sauna and shower. The marble sink top and supporting brackets are antiques that match existing ones in the house. The faucet is a reproduction by Sunrise Specialties.

Keeping fixtures and wall tile white contributes to the period feeling, as does the mixture of genuinely antique with new. For instance, the sconces are old, while the ceiling fixture is a reproduction, nickel-plated by its manufacturer, Restoration Lamp & Fixture. The room's details and colors reference utilitarian period rooms rather than parlors or other formal spaces.

MASTER BATHROOM

This bathroom, a converted trunk room, adjoins the upstairs sitting room and master bedroom. It feels more stylish than the original bathroom, thanks to a marble floor, a small claw-foot tub (in addition to the tiled shower) and decorative period accessories. The sink, sink brackets and lighting fixtures are antiques, while Chicago Faucet made the nickel-plated faucets. The walls feature a gray blue popular in the 1890s. The stained trim is original, as are the Japanesque sliding louvers.

Jean Dunbar is a consultant and writer specializing in period interiors. Her award-winning design work has appeared in major national magazines. Peter Sils owns and operates Sils Construction, Inc., a fifteen-person firm with special expertise in the rehabilitation of historic buildings.

APPLIANCES: EVOLUTION AFTER THE REVOLUTION

By John M. Jowers

The Victorian home, inside and out, was an elaborate architectural assembly of decorative and detailed woodwork. The kitchens in these homes, however, remained a workplace for the house staff, a place not to be seen by the visiting public. The sir or madam of the house seldom ventured into this room, thus there was no need for elaborate furnishings. The typical Victorian kitchen featured a cooking center, food preparation area, food storage area and a sink area for cleanup. Cooking centers were of four types or designs: the open fire design, the box stove, the wood and coal stove, and the gas stove.

The open-fire design was no more than a large, open fireplace with swing-out hooks for pot cooking and an oven encased in the rock or brick structure of the fireplace to allow for baking. Open-fire cooking centers such as this were the norm for centuries prior to the Victorian period but continued as part of many Victorian homes until the 1880s. These open-fire cooking areas were large, messy, hot and very labor intensive. During this period, even middle-class homes employed a servant staff to fulfill the task of food preparation.

The box stove, though introduced in Europe in the 1750s, made its debut in the colonies around 1880. These large stoves were some 6 feet wide and 6 feet tall with a partitioned firebox connected to several ovens and cooking surfaces by means of air-baffled chambers. By adjusting the heat flow from the oven to various parts of the stove, temperatures could be regulated to accommodate different types of cooking. This was a very labor-intensive contraption to operate, requiring constant attention not only to keep the smaller fire going but to ensure proper temperatures throughout the stove. A proficient chef knew how to move utensils from one location of the stove to another to achieve the perfect cooking results.

(opposite and above) *Mid- to late-nineteenth-century stoves offered greater efficiency than hearth cooking. They were also objects of great beauty.*

These stoves required venting to the outside by means of a chimney or vent flue.

The wood and coal stove gained popularity in the late 1880s. It was a much smaller appliance than the open-fire centers and the box stoves, yet it, too, required constant attention to maintain proper temperatures. These units were generally freestanding in design, available with either a low wrap base design or a base with short, curved legs. The fireboxes in these stoves were very small with a small ash dump pan below the firebox. These ash pans required daily cleaning to ensure a proper fire. Because of the smaller, more compact design of these stoves, fewer people were required to prepare a meal, and thus kitchen staffs began to dwindle. In the 1890s and at the turn of the century, many stove makers began fitting these

(left) *Although a major step up in convenience from open-hearth cooking, wood stoves still needed constant tending. They continued to be a regular part of rural life well into the twentieth century. Today, people often rehabilitate antique stoves or purchase those designed to look old, but fabricated with twenty-first century technology. This lovely example of a period piece lives in the kitchen of a northern Mississippi farmhouse.*

(opposite page) *This great, old stove is no longer used for cooking but is cherished as a family heirloom antique and is part of the décor of this new log house.*

wood and coal stoves with gas rails and burners. This transformed the kitchen stove into a more efficient cooking apparatus, one even the madam of the house could attend.

Although many of these first-generation stoves left the food with a hint of gas flavor, the cleaner fire and instant heat was a welcome trade. It took manufacturers only a few years to address the odor and taste issue.

Gas stoves from the late 1890s and the turn of the century were quite elaborate with intricately designed nickel trim work. The "Victorian Trivet" was used as an ornamental application on the fronts of many of these stoves.

WITH THE ADVENT OF ELECTRICITY

In 1893, one of the first electric stoves made its appearance at the World's Columbian Exposition. Although there were several other experimental models around at the time, all were considered crude by design as well as unpredictable to operate. With electricity being limited primarily to areas in and around larger cities, the demand for these stoves was limited as well.

Most electric stoves were designed and sold for commercial applications. By 1907, however, the Edison Electric Company (later General Electric) offered a full line of electric cooking gadgets. The first residentially designed stove to be marketed by Edison was a cooking table. This table design device consisted of a large, flat surface with several shelves positioned above and below.

The cooking table had a row of electrical outlets that allowed for the plugging in of various appliances. A fully outfitted cooking table was equipped with several hotplate-style cooking units, simmering or chaffing dishes, coffee urns and small ovens.

The benefit of the electric cooking table was seen mostly in the elimination of the open flame. Though greatly reducing the heat generated throughout the cooking area, these units were very unsightly with their tangled web of electrical cords running from this place to that.

The first self-contained electric stove was introduced by Hughes Electric Company in 1910. This stove was clean by design, resembling the presentation of similar gas stoves of the day. Offered in a black cabinet with heavy nickel trim, this electric stove also offered concealed wiring, cleaning up its appearance from previous contraptions. As modern and

twentieth century as this electric stove was, sale of the stove was still greatly limited by the availability of electricity itself.

TRANSITION TO EFFICIENCY & STORAGE

The food-preparation area of the Victorian kitchen consisted of nothing more than a large wooden table, usually located in the center of the kitchen. Though primarily used for food processing, these tables became the central workspace for other household chores. It has been said, "The kitchen is the heart of the home." This statement was never truer than during the Victorian period. As the country enjoyed the fruits of economic growth, the demand for improved modern conveniences sparked a literal industrial revolution for the Victorian kitchen. With an increase in material goods for the home, the need for more efficient means to maintain such items escalated as well. In the past, the sole purpose of the kitchen was to prepare the day's meals. The servants' routine now included care of lace, lamp chimneys, glassware, tin ware, silverware, candles, even clothing and furniture. With more to do in a day, the need for a more efficient kitchen was a must. It is no wonder this central worktable began to find itself covered with gadgets of all types used to assist in the daily operation and cleaning of these large homes.

Food-storage areas of the Victorian kitchen generally consisted of an assortment of bins and baskets that held everything from vegetables to flour and grains. Prior to the 1880s, food preservation remained a process of salting, smoking or pickling. With the availability of electricity in larger populated areas, the icebox became a popular addition. By the mid-1880s, many affluent homeowners were adding an icebox to their otherwise sparsely furnished kitchen. A 100-pound block of ice could provide a chilled storage temperature of 40 degrees in these insulated boxes for up to a week. The first-generation iceboxes were constructed from oak, then lined with tin and fitted with a system of shelves. Several doors installed on the front of the cabinet allowed convenient access to items stored within. A center shelf near the top was designed to accommodate the size and weight of the ice block. As cold air by nature settles to the bottom, locating the ice near the top allowed for natural cooling and air circulation throughout the box.

The owners of this early Indiana Victorian went to great pains to maintain as much of the house's history in their kitchen as possible. Note their antique icebox.

Beneath the ice-block shelf a shallow tray was located to catch the water as the block melted. The drip tray was then fitted with a small drain hose that lead to a larger pan under the icebox. The larger pan required periodic emptying. With chilled storage now available in the home, the Victorian kitchen had become the most efficient kitchen to date.

MIGHT AS WELL INCLUDE THE SINK

The kitchen sink has been around for centuries. Although most water used in these sinks was hauled to the kitchen in buckets, by the later part of the Victorian period, running water was available. The first kitchen sinks to utilize running water usually did so with a hand pump that drew the water from a well. In some instances, these wells were located directly under the home. Progress came quickly and by the late 1880s, running water throughout the Victorian home was the norm, being delivered by lever-controlled faucets much like those we use today.

For centuries, food preparation and cooking was a task that began at sunrise and ended at sunset, with most chores being done the same way for centuries. Throughout the Victorian era, more changes evolved in this daily process than in any period before. While the introduction of gas and electric cooking stoves, as well as insulated iceboxes, led to tremendous changes in the operation of the Victorian kitchen, even these modern improvements seem crude by today's standards. It would be during the years following the Great Depression that American kitchens would begin a transformation that included built-in cabinets, fully self-contained cooking appliances and electric refrigerators in a room that truly became a part of the home.

John M. Jowers is president of AntiqueAppliances.com, one of the nation's leading antique appliance restoration shops. Mr. Jowers is a nationally recognized authority on large antique appliances.

BATHROOMS: A SHORT HISTORY

From the earliest Victorian Neo-classical and Rococo revival house in the second and third quarters of the nineteenth century, on through to the Arts and Crafts period of the early twentieth century, the facilities, style and design of the bathroom underwent major changes. The critical issue, of course, was plumbing. The earliest houses, but for makeshift privies and other machinations, generally did not have sewage systems. Bathrooms were just that—rooms or parts of rooms where family members bathed. Tubs were often in the kitchen or in other tucked-away areas of the home. Sometimes there were specific rooms for that purpose. It was fairly hit-and-miss. During the late Victorian years, bathrooms—often called water closets—became an integral part of the house.

Originally, bedrooms featured the typical decorative basin and pitcher for washing and shaving. Later bathrooms incorporated those features as well and the basin was actually set into a washstand. That washstand eventually included pipes for draining. Over the years, backsplash tiles were set into the walls and sinks became less independent pieces resembling furniture and took on a more familiar appearance. Drainage systems were also included in bathtubs and voila—came the bathroom as we know it today.

Almost every community in America has a Victorian museum house that was *the* nineteenth-century home of the local majordomo who, as its proud curator will state, "Was the first man in this community to put in indoor plumbing."

Certainly, the wealthiest people in the third quarter of the nineteenth century considered their bathrooms symbols that they had arrived, knowing that their more middle-class cousins were still making midnight trips outside or using the services of the chamber pot.

Although the first flush toilets allegedly were used in Crete four thousand years ago, there was no consistency in sanitation systems anywhere, least of all the New World. There's an old nursery rhyme that, while not necessarily universally true, fairly well conveys the facts up until the mid-nineteenth century:

> *In days of old, when knights were bold*
> *And toilets weren't invented,*
> *They left their load by the side of the road*
> *And walked away contented.*

There's a fascination with toilets that goes well beyond kindergarten humor and makes the toilet stand alone among historians and archeologists. In fact, there's the Sulabh International Museum of Toilets in New Delhi, India. The museum traces the history of the toilet for the last 4,500 years. One of the founders is Dr. Bindeswar Pathak, Ph.D., D.Litt., who stated, "The toilet is a part of the history of human hygiene that is a critical chapter in the history of human civilization and which cannot be isolated to be accorded an unimportant position in history. Toilet is a critical link between order and disorder and between good and bad environment . . . the more developed was the society, the more sanitized it became and vice versa."

THE TOILET COMES OF AGE

As the flush toilet gained popularity in the latter part of the nineteenth century, the bathroom took on its own persona. There was no consistency in bathroom design or décor. There were those that were most plain, using white, sanitary-appearing subway tile, having the simplified basics; there were others that were as ornately embellished as the other high-Victorian rooms of the house, replete with oriental rugs, furniture, stained glass, wallpaper and artwork. Even experts disagree on what was typical.

The bathroom, even then, often needed to be a pretty place. By gosh, if the community kingpin was going to have a bathroom, he was going to include a beautifully embossed and decorated toilet, exotic hardwoods as wainscoting, a handmade stained-glass window by Belcher, the latest in elaborate period lighting and vanity tables. Floors were rarely wood, but if so, they were often painted. Mostly they had colorful mosaics made of three-quarter-inch square or hexagon tiles or sometimes even encaustic tile. The kingpin and his family were flush with their newfound wealth and not only wanted to enjoy it, but show it off.

THE BASICS AND BEYOND

For the general middle-class public whose homes were not part of the local A-list, and unless the homeowner had the desire to go over the top, the bathroom was quite ordinary, with a cast-iron tub; an independent, free-standing sink; toilet; and perhaps a matching bidet.

As the middle class grew and plumbers became an industry unto themselves, so came a variety of bathrooms from the opulent to the basic. Even the Prince of Wales, before the turn of the century, was noted to have stated, "Were I not a prince, I'd like to be a plumber."

Not until the Arts and Crafts movement was there any impetus to focus design on matching cabinetry and woodwork. Even then, it was most often the exception rather than the rule that the bathroom would incorporate any of the mission-style woodwork integrated in the rest of the house. Individual pieces of furniture and fixtures were standard, and it wasn't until decades later (well into the twentieth century) that consistent wall-to-wall cabinetry and countertops were part of the overall bathroom design. Donald Hooper, owner of Vintage Plumbing and something of a toiletologist, addresses the use of bathroom fixtures in the Victorian period:

Embossed toilets epitomize the artistry and decorativeness of the Victorian-era bathroom. In my opinion, anyone re-creating a true Victorian-era bathroom must include a toilet that has embossed decoration. It makes no difference if the tank is a high-on-the-wall pull-chain tank, or a low tank near the bowl. It could be wood (usually oak, but many other hard woods were also available) or china. These toilets came in sets with any type of tank.

Trade catalogs were the primary means that were used to learn what items were available. These catalogs were lavishly produced with the finest illustrations to display their goods, and buyers would select the fixtures they liked from these catalogs.

Toilets would have figural raised or embossed decorations cast onto them, such as a lion head, or a dolphin or a lion paw, or more commonly they would have floral décor, like a garland or a vine design growing up from the base. Some bowls had a basket weave design on the sides with a floral embellishment right in front. Sometimes the decorations were hand painted in gold leaf before they were fired in the kiln. (In 1859 Queen Victoria's toilet was decorated with gold, and in 1883 she enjoyed the very first ceramic toilet bowl.)

Small touches, like the Eastlake towel rack, the period-style soap dish and the mirror, finish out this bathroom that has major Victorian design features such as wainscoting.

Most people equate oak with antique bathrooms, especially toilet tanks. But oak was the cheap wood used in fixtures sold to the masses. Far more exotic woods were used in fine Victorian bathrooms, with bird's-eye maple being perhaps the most rare and expensive, other than some rare African woods.

In the high-Victorian home, if the bathroom was designed to reflect the rest of the house's interior, then it was often done that way with a vengeance. As toilets were embellished beyond anything reasonable for a utilitarian fixture with one simple operation, it was clearly to disguise what superficially prurient Victorians considered an unmentionable bodily function.

It was also during this integration of the complete bathroom in the late 1800s that the tub as the main source of body cleansing was rivaled by the showerhead. Various forms of showers began being advertised as stalls or attachments to the tub.

As Victorian houses went through their various incarnations over the decades, the bathrooms suffered the most as chipped tiles were not replaced, plumbing broke and was not properly—or aesthetically—repaired, wallpaper peeled and cheap linoleum was applied as the floor covering. Eventually, when remodeling was undertaken, it was with an eye toward expense and simplicity. The claw-foot tub was replaced with an enameled tub that was attached to the walls; white became the universal obligatory color.

It is said, with the bath as well as the kitchen, that one can't describe a home's interior décor based on the design of either of those rooms. It isn't only because they are the costliest to refurbish but also because most of the cost is hidden behind walls. Remodeling these rooms perhaps might be first on our wish lists but last in our practical financial priorities. They are also the rooms that we can least afford to do without while they are in the process of being remodeled.

As the twentieth century progressed, color schemes and interior design changed, but by and large the basics of plumbing remain the same. Today we have the opportunity, with jetted tubs, showers with multiple heads, and bathrooms incorporating steam baths and saunas, to return to another era. We can use the same principles of design for Victoriana—and then some—to enjoy a period of timeless sensuality the Victorians, despite their protestations, really seemed to understand.

One of the early bathrooms adjacent to a bedroom in a period-Victorian house.

Elegant wallpaper and woodworking typified the robber baron mentality. Even in the bathroom, "mine is more luxurious than yours" was the design motto of the era.

CITY & COUNTRY KITCHENS

In the mid-to late nineteenth century and into the early twentieth century, high-Victorian-style houses with turrets, gingerbread, tall ceilings, multi-patterned wallpapers and lushly carved furniture were de rigueur among the middle and wealthy classes in cities and towns. At the same time, farming and pioneering families built far smaller houses in the rural communities throughout the country. Architecturally, farmhouses of that era were less ornate and had lower ceilings, smaller windows and fewer rooms. Most of these households were run by the family, most often the woman of the house, without servants. The country kitchen was then—as it is today—an integrated part of the house, while the city kitchen was a basement denizen haunted by pale, sun-deprived domestics ruled by the mistress of the house much the way Queen Victoria ruled her empire.

(below) *This kitchen is in the childhood home of President Harry Truman near Independence, Missouri. A simple farmhouse of the late Victorian era, it offers the kind of uncomplicated but compelling ambiance that draws so many to the Victorian farmhouse look. This might be the place where Truman coined the phrase, "If you can't stand the heat, get out of the kitchen."*

(opposite) *This kitchen in the Charles Ramsey house in St. Paul, Minnesota, is pure city Victorian with clean lines and uncluttered spaces.*

While the kitchen of the mid- to large-size Victorian city house was probably larger than those smaller farmhouses, the working basics were similar. Despite their tall ceilings, these rooms were hot in the summer and still poorly ventilated in the winter. Mostly they were stark, unadorned and uncomfortable.

Cooking was no picnic in either of those situations. The only benefit to living in a city house was if you were the woman of the house, you probably didn't spend long hours in the kitchen. City kitchen or country kitchen, whoever did the cooking in those years was working hard and long hours to bring food to the table.

COUNTRY COOKIN'

The kitchens of rural Victorian-era homes are not entirely unlike what one might find in a rustically designed country-style cabin of today, minus twenty-first-century appliances and conveniences. The look was wood or whitewashed walls, basic open shelving and simple wooden furniture. Those early cabins and cottages still inspire feelings of primitive coziness and provide the intrinsic appeal that drives twenty-first-century second-home buyers and builders to construct new cabins and cottages or to rehabilitate old ones. The basic draw of the Victorian farmhouse, especially its kitchen, lies in the simplicity of its look and design and the beguiling supposition of a less-complicated lifestyle.

Even toy makers of the Victorian era represented accurate portrayals of late-nineteenth-century kitchens. This one-of-a-kind dollhouse created in the shelves of a Victorian lawyer's bookcase shows what each of the rooms in a city Victorian town house would have looked like at the time. Note the open hearth, pine floors and worktable.

52
✳ ✳ ✳ ✳

For those who want a high-style Victorian kitchen, one that emulates the embellished Victorian design palette, there is no historically accurate pattern to follow. In re-creating the Victorian kitchen of a period house, the key word is *create,* because the kitchen look we are after never really existed. So, instead of borrowing much more than the high ceilings and long windows from period kitchens, we take decorating cues from the more public rooms of Victorian homes.

We can now have our Victorian cake and eat it too. We can decide to create the simple and rustic farmhouse kitchen, go with the almost-contemporary-looking whitewashed simplicity of the Victorian city kitchen as it was, or use design concepts borrowed from Victorian parlors to make the Victorian-style kitchen and bathroom that most appeal to us.

EITHER OR

If ornate hand-carved wood, rich dark walnut-stained cabinetry, elegant textiles, tall ceilings, and walls with long windows appeal to you, city Victorian style is probably the right look for your kitchen. It will be a more sophisticated overall design that will probably include marble or stone countertops and seamless matching cabinetry with carved molding and trim that reaches the ceiling. Elaborate ceiling friezes, boldly painted walls, wallpaper and/or borders also hearken to the upscale Victorian aesthetic. With a nod to the challenges of cooking that create some steam, grease and smoke, if the Victorians put it in the parlor, you can put it in the kitchen.

If it is the elemental Victorian farmhouse style that is appealing, the unfitted kitchen is appropriate. It will include freestanding furnishings such as Hoosier cabinets, oak tables and chairs, and either antique or reproduction stoves and refrigerators. Style- and period-appropriate textiles are cotton and other natural fibers. The all-over ambiance is one of freshness and informality of the sort found in country-style décor.

While the differences between country and city Victorian design are quite pronounced, there are some common design elements that can be

Copper pots, unfitted standing cupboards and a well-worn worktable make this a kitchen that has a historic ambiance with a twenty-first-century appeal. There is nothing in this kitchen that could not be emulated in a contemporary house, and probably for a lot less money than the price of kitchen showroom materials.

especially well applied to all period kitchens, including wainscoting, the use of stained (as opposed to painted) wood trim and natural materials, and historically appropriate lighting that is either antique or well-produced reproduction-style pieces of the era. Natural materials in flooring such as wood, tile or brick might have been found in both and are also prime for use in producing a twenty-first-century-style Victorian kitchen.

There are kitchens that are blends of the two styles with twenty-first-century elements such as stainless steel appliances and high-tech industrial lighting to balance the look. Straddling three centuries can produce dynamic design. In short, Victorian kitchen design can be about high style, home style or a blend done with the true Victorian soul—combining some or all of it to suit the individual style of the homeowner. ❀

(this page) *This simple bathroom with its washstand and mirror would have been typical of such a room in a farmhouse.*

(opposite page) *This is the ultimate Victorian farm kitchen. Photographed at the original Laura Ingalls Wilder homestead in DeSmet, South Dakota, it is easy to picture Laura and her family preparing a meal. With the family piano, cook stove, dresser and eating/food prep table, this room represents the family kitchen of rural Victorian homes.*

(this page) *This nineteenth-century country farm kitchen in a Mississippi dogtrot incorporates simple textiles, an unfitted cabinet, pale-toned yellow walls, pine floors and a butcher-block table that are still appealing today. This kitchen could be then or now.*

(opposite page) *From country simplicity to city sophistication: these homeowners took a cue from their more public Victorian rooms when they renovated the kitchen. Note floral wallpaper, warm wood cabinets and granite counter-tops. This is definitely a twenty-first-century take on Victorian sensibilities.*

In the bathroom as well as the kitchen, the use of simple and unfitted materials was typical of the era. Board door and log walls date to the Victorian era.

What Makes It Victorian

✳ ✳

Borrowing from Other Design Traditions

Both in authentic museum houses built in the mid- to late nineteenth century and in the refurbishing of private houses of the era, one may walk into the kitchen or any other room of the house and be amazed at the amalgam of trims, moldings and seemingly odd combinations of wood embellishments. The first reaction might be that they did it wrong. One would be tempted to think, "It's not Victorian, it's Federal," or "That's not Victorian, it's Greek revival." The fact is the Victorians borrowed from the architectural styles of other eras, mixing them as they saw fit and enjoyed.

FUNNY, IT DOESN'T LOOK VICTORIAN
By Victoria Imperioli

The Victorian era was a period in architecture and decorative arts that witnessed the most intense confluence of all previous styles and tastes and merged to create the look of Victorian splendor and ingenuity. High-Victorian style was born out of the revivals. A typical Victorian residence could boast Italianate, Regency, Gothic and other styles under a single roof, seemingly creating a cacophony of the styles, but Victorians knew just how to incorporate all these elements into a single scheme.

The Victorian era also means industrialization and mass production. It marks a period of "balloon construction," which implies that moldings and other architectural elements would no longer be molded into place individually, or carved one by one. Rather they would come in strips and be shipped from factories in bulk. The industrialization of the decorative crafts further implied that the materials used were no longer traditional wood and plaster; instead less expensive materials were sought to replace them.

Almost as early as the time of Adam, composition materials mixed with rabbit-skin glue would be used in place of plaster. The mechanization of the Victorian era brought the mass production of architectural elements to yet another level. Victorian moldings would be produced in wood, plaster, papier-mâché, tin paper and, above all, composition materials. Often gesso would be used as an outer layer above the composition material of choice to create the raised surface detail. Fibrous plaster was employed as well as the lightweight anaglyphic paper and borders. Early catalogs of the era listed hundreds of moldings in various styles and materials.

Naturally, the rooms of greatest social importance in a residence would be the most embellished and ornate. The parlor, the study, the dining room and other prominent rooms had opulent moldings and wall hangings. The rooms of secondary importance such as the breakfast room, bedrooms, the morning room, etc., frequently had none of these decorative elements.

From furnishings to architecture, this room is pure Victorian.

61

✳ ✳ ✳ ✳ ✳

The opulence of the public rooms of period-Victorian houses cannot be overstated. Ceilings were painted or papered, along with the portion of the wall that extended to the picture railing. In these highly decorated rooms were elaborate cornices that were used to complete the style of ceilings of the chosen design. Gothic reproductions or the opulent Baroque moldings that paid homage to the gilded era adorned ceiling designs. Even in this grand décor, they relied on composition materials in some of the most splendid houses in England. We must always keep in mind that as much as they wished to preserve their ties with the canons and traditions of the past, Victorians were part of a modern industrialized society.

So while the use of highly ornate trim materials might not have been found in the kitchens of even the grandest Victorian mansions, it certainly gives modern-day Victorians who are creating their versions of nineteenth-century kitchens license to borrow a variety of styles of trim, moldings and other design elements from earlier eras and still be well within an appropriate and accurate design aesthetic.

Victoria Imperioli is the president of SVE Designs, New York City, and has rehabilitated two nineteenth-century New York City historic buildings. Her home was recently featured on the cover and interior pages of Architectural Digest.

MAKING IT THE VICTORIAN WAY

There's little more daunting when planning to refurbish or create a Victorian kitchen than to look at it in its entirety and become aware of how huge an undertaking it really is. However, when we pull it apart piece by piece, project by project, the endeavor appears less monumental. Doing or redoing a kitchen in this way also allows us to take it one step at a time as money, energy and time become available.

Victoriana didn't necessarily end with the evolution of the simpler, cleaner, less embellished lines of the Arts and Crafts movement. Nor did it end with Art Nouveau or even the modernist era of the 1950s. Many facets of Victoriana remain standards of house design even now.

However, the further we get from the nineteenth and earliest parts of the twentieth centuries, the more that era fuses with other periods. Unless one is focused on historical accuracy, the specifics of Victoriana are difficult to define. In the same way that historic museum houses of the Victorian period might contain furniture from the earlier Empire or even Federal periods, it's entirely acceptable in your Victorian kitchen to borrow items from the later Depression era, such as colorful utensils, small and large appliances, and serving ware to fill out the room. After all, houses are multigenerational and it is acceptable to use materials from a variety of design periods.

LET ME COUNT THE WAYS
By Susan Dean

Ah, the Victorian kitchen—filled with the scents of home-baked bread and simmering soups or stews, dominated by a wood-burning stove shining with nickel-plated trim, its wooden floors gleaming, its open shelves sagging under the weight of handsome yellow ware and granite-ware, and canned or packaged goods with artistically lithographed labels.

For most of the nineteenth century, storage in kitchens and pantries was usually on open shelves, where pots and pans kept out in the open picked up greasy cooking fumes; food that wasn't eaten within a day or two of its purchase was in danger of spoiling and—uh-oh, was that a mouse scampering away behind the apple barrel?

Perhaps it would be wiser to forget about authenticity in the kitchen and think instead about creating the illusion of the past with choices that add old-fashioned charm and the aura of some generic yesterday. By judiciously mixing old and new you can have the best of both worlds.

The truth is that a real nineteenth-century kitchen was austere in design and the most under-decorated room in the house. The true Victorian kitchen was hot, steamy and smelly, a model of uncomfortable inconvenience and inefficiency, a room in which one would not want to be forced to prepare three meals a day. However, if one suspends all senses but sight when regarding these spaces, there is a visual charm in their plainness and simplicity. Beauty speaks to all of us differently. Whitewashed plaster walls, nickel-trimmed stoves and honed-wood surfaces of floors and worktables appeal to lovers of contemporary minimalist design. Given modern cooking appliances, ventilation and other conveniences, it is as valid a part of Victorian décor as the more opulent, colorful and dramatic ornamentation found in the rest of the house of that period.

Still, for most passionate lovers of things Victorian, this style is just too stark. They would likely prefer to apply to their kitchens the bolder and more colorful elements of Victorian décor that were found in period parlors.

This is actually a period-Victorian kitchen, but it can easily be created in a new space. A pale wall color and white-plus-pewter tones are historically accurate and simple. The metal-topped farm table and a few well-placed antique pieces create design that is appealing to Victorian purists as well as those who prefer style that is more contemporary. Beyond that, this room could never look dated because everything in it is of the period.

WHAT MAKES IT VICTORIAN

These homeowners opted for an ultra-simple approach when they refurbished the kitchen of their nineteenth-century house. Here, they chose period-appropriate shutters as their sole window treatment.

Old-World stove and brick floor give Victorian style to this new house.

In either case, there are a number of ways to achieve your preferred vision of the Victorian kitchen aesthetic—with relative ease. These suggestions can also extend to include the bathroom, if you desire Victorian ambiance there. Several projects are actually do-it-yourself at relatively low cost. Some are true to period design while others are Fictorian (period design fiction but suggestive of the era). All are valid when the goal is to suggest Victorian décor.

1. If you are remodeling a house, consider installing a pine floor and then painting it. Although laying the floor will most likely need to be done by professionals, painting it can be done by almost anyone. The paint job will add a late-nineteenth-century look to the kitchen, providing a large dose of visual drama for the cost of a weekend and paint supplies.

2. Heavy-duty linoleum, which has been around for more than a hundred years, will also add authenticity to a floor; it is also less costly than hardwood flooring. If you have a plywood subfloor, you can also consider painting that—not a bad idea for a bathroom.

3. Tiling your floor also provides a period-Victorian design element. Tile became de rigueur in late-nineteenth-century kitchens once the notion of germs and sanitation entered into the equation of home building.

4. Not necessarily authentic, but somehow of the Victorian style, braided and rag rugs placed on the kitchen floor will also give a Victorian feeling for very little financial investment. They also help tired feet; what a scullery maid would have done for one!

5. Chair rail and wainscoting send an immediate visual cue that the space is historically accurate Victorian. One can either paint a color that will extend to the ceiling above the wainscoting or select wallpaper that will be easy to live with when you are cooking three meals a day.

6. You can even splurge with one or several fabulous historic Victorian wallpapers provided in one of numerous wallpaper catalogs. Most companies can tell you which wallpaper patterns in their catalog work well together.

With the addition of fretwork to the tops of kitchen cabinets and the vintage-appearing lace trim to shelves, this kitchen offers accents of Victorian design without being necessarily historically authentic.

This simple freestanding Victorian cabinet works perfectly in this small bathroom and adds the perfect note of period style in a Williamsport, Pennsylvania, Victorian.

7. Painted walls with a painted, stenciled or wallpapered border that extends down several inches from the ceiling are design appropriate, relatively inexpensive and another do-it-yourself project that will render the kitchen or bath Victorian.

8. The ceiling is a blank canvas where expansive décor might be a bit subtler than opulent walls. Consider the talents of local artists or art students whose fresco-style work might lend a unique design flavor to the ceiling of your kitchen or bathroom.

9. Pull-down shades and shutters were the most standard window treatment in period-Victorian kitchens and baths. They still do the job, again for relatively little money, and can be homeowner installed.

10. Add gingerbread trim and other fretwork to the corners of windows and doorways. They are available precut at most major home department stores and are now made incredibly easy to install. It will instantly identify the space as Victorian. If you don't mind the challenge of working with original materials (or you have a good carpenter), architectural salvage firms have good supplies of trim. Actually, you can find original materials at flea markets, antiques malls—just about everywhere.

11. Instead of using all built-in cabinetry, opt for either an antique or reproduc-

The period Hoosier cabinet is just the right piece for this period-Virginia farmhouse.

A pie safe is another of the highly collectible antique furnishings that are period appropriate in a nineteenth-century kitchen. Given the cost of high-quality, newly manufactured or even custom-crafted cabinetry, antique pieces are often as affordable as new ones and offer greater charm and authenticity to the room.

tion Hoosier cabinet or pie safe, typically found in late-nineteenth-century kitchens.

12. Use bead board, pine or oak built-in cabinets if there is no room for freestanding furniture.

13. Add moldings and old-fashioned hinges and pulls to new cabinetry for an instant shot of Victorian style.

14. Try glass-fronted cabinets with shelves trimmed in lace, fringe or other edging; it's not historic Victorian but adds a feeling of the era.

15. Instead of an island, consider a long farmer's worktable, either antique or reproduction. If you really need the storage, add baskets below to hold small appliances and even potatoes and onions. If you can't find a table you love, try your hand at making your own out of a pine top and premade turned legs from a home supply store. The cost is minimal compared to antiques, so you have only a little time invested in a large item that adds considerable Victorian style.

16. Both antique and reproduction lighting are available in almost every

The large corbel used as a shelf, the Victorian hanging cupboard, and curved armchair are all late-nineteenth-century design elements.

This period Victorian has utilized many design options to maintain a nineteenth-century-appearing kitchen. Elements include the tall cabinets, vintage cook stove, freestanding cupboard and the shelf, created by placing a decorative board across antique corbels.

budget range. Most experts agree that this is the place to spend a little money. You really get what you pay for in terms of authentic design style. No matter the financial investment, remember that if you select a bowl-shaped fixture, make sure the bottom of the bowl is over the table, the open portion at the top, or you'll find yourself staring into bare lightbulbs every time you look upward.

17. Display your collections of small antiques and china on shelves made by placing a board across corbels or other Victorian architec-

tural design elements. This may not be authentic, but it will still suggest Victorian décor. Wide corbels can even be used as shelves for small items. This is another weekend design project that is both inexpensive and easy.

Susan Dean, a native New Yorker, has spent her career writing for magazines, including Victorian Decorating, Victorian Decorating & Lifestyles, Country Accents, Decorating Solutions *and* Paint Magic.

MOLDING, TRIM & WAINSCOTING

Although there is no requirement to dot every *i* in creating Victorian ambiance in our kitchens and bathrooms, it's important at least to know the parameters of what is period appropriate. How far each of us wants to utilize that information is, of course, freewill, but knowing about the details that bring together the bigger picture can be an invaluable tool.

Molding and trim that incorporate decorative carving is to a room what a frame is to a picture. One would not have an aluminum frame around a Renaissance painting or a Victorian-carved frame surrounding a contemporary collage. Frames, in and of themselves, have reached a new stature in the worlds of art and antiques. They are now looked upon as artwork and are commanding prices often rivaling—if not surpassing—the artworks they support. Surprise—surprise: the artists and artisans who created those frames were well aware of their aesthetic value. So it is with moldings that add a quality of dimension that creates an entire picture.

MILLWORK
By Brent Hull

The height of the Victorian era is truly the golden age of architectural millwork. Wood was cheap and plentiful and the machine age suddenly allowed for an incredible variety of bold and creative moldings that no longer had to be hand carved. That dramatic millwork changed the face of home design.

Unlike the Victorian kitchen, the bathroom was a status symbol, the number of bathrooms in a house equating to rank and prestige. In contrast to the kitchen, baths were often richly adorned and beautifully tiled.

Despite the fact that a period-Victorian kitchen was rarely "decorated" in the same sense that a parlor might have been, millwork always played a large role in the look and efficiency of the space. Utilitarian as it was intended to be, millwork was still often carefully and beautifully crafted. Today, no matter how fancy or plain the rest of kitchen décor might be, the re-creation of any Victorian-style kitchen will require attention to millwork detail.

The Louisiana owners of a true late-nineteenth-century house created an elegant new kitchen family living space by wisely investing time and budget on fine wood moldings and trims that frame the entire area.

IT'S ALL IN THE DETAILS

Since a modern kitchen's storage space may comprise 75 percent of the wall space, cabinet design details are crucial to establishing at least a feeling of historic authenticity, to say nothing of contemporary usability. In order to emulate the cabinetry of a period kitchen, the doors must sit flush with the face frame of the cabinet. This allows for the use of period-style hardware and gives the cabinets a furniture-quality look. Modern overlay cabinet doors are a post–World War II invention and thus have no place in a Victorian-style kitchen.

The choice and cut of wood for historic-style millwork is also pertinent. When softwoods were used in a true period kitchen, they most often were painted. Re-creating that element of Victorian style therefore is easy.

Because of the advancements of modern machinery after the 1870s, the availability of hardwood moldings and finer details in wood millwork greatly increased. If a hardwood was used, it was most likely quartersawn and rift-sawn white oak. The manner in which the wood is cut determines the grain pattern on the face of the board. Plain-sawn oak today doesn't come close to resembling millwork of the late 1800s and early 1900s. The quality of timber was much higher and thus the grain patterns were tighter and more uniform. That is why using rift- and quartersawn oak today is so important in maintaining a historic look. Other historically appropriate stain-grade woods are cherry, walnut and even bird's-eye maple, though rift- and quartersawn oak are most popular.

SIZE, SPACE & PROPORTION

Cabinet arrangement is another key element in kitchen design because it can define spaces and their usage. The historic kitchen was quite small because it was thought to be more efficient for work. Modern kitchens are larger and have an easier flow. To bridge this size gap in designing a historic-style kitchen, it helps to use cabinet groupings to create a sense of place, like the breakfast nook or the butler's pantry and serving area.

Historic cabinets were often site built even up into the 1920s and '30s. The built-ins of the Victorian age were much more decorative and would have been placed in areas of importance to show off. Kitchen cabinets were not even included in trade catalogs until the early 1920s and then it was more the doors for the site-built cases. This is important to remember because it helps accurately lay out groupings; for instance, the butler's pantry piece can be more decorative than other areas.

Not only are the cabinets and trims of period feeling, but the drawer pulls and cabinet hinges are of period style as well.

(above) *This Louisiana kitchen (see image on page 68) even continues the wood paneling onto the stove hood and wraps the entire space in warm-feeling cabinetry and window trim.*

(left) *In the same Louisiana kitchen, the fine trims, moldings and cabinetry are extended into an adjoining open and spacious dining area.*

(top left) *The bead board and clean, straight lines of cabinets, simple trim and lower-slung cabinetry are period accurate in this Little Rock, Arkansas, house.*

(top right) *Also typical of the Arts and Crafts period are the hammered metal drawer and cabinet pulls.*

(bottom left) *This dining area of a period Arts and Crafts house in Asheville, North Carolina, uses the simple, clean lines of the early twentieth century in moldings, trims and cabinetry.*

ORNAMENTATION

One of the most dramatic design elements that identifies the Victorian era is ornate trims and moldings. Modern machinery enabled artisans to be highly decorative with carvings and applied moldings. Because machine-made moldings were so cheap, there were usually more of them; they were often applied on top of one another. The shapes were bold and could be either gothic or classical in nature, depending on the architectural style.

Victorian-style moldings are easy to identify. Highly ornate and decorative, with many cut faces and details, they often make use of rosettes and plinth blocks on doors and windows. Those made in the Victorian era can be identified because they are machine made from hardwood. The sheer number of moldings will often identify their historic period.

By contrast, in pre–Industrial Revolution colonial houses, only the very high-style homes featured ornate moldings because they were so expensive to make by hand. Further, because they were handmade, only softwoods could be used for this purpose to any great extent in the Colonial era.

In re-creating the ambiance of a Victorian kitchen, one should compare the classical proportions of the size of millwork to the piece being decorated and take off from there. It's a great way to have fun with the look.

BATHROOM MILLWORK

Within the framework of millwork in the Victorian house, kitchens and bathrooms were such different spaces from each other that they can't be re-created the same way if period accuracy is the goal. Each had its own design and transitional period for incorporating new décor and technology.

The period-Victorian bathroom was not an area where millwork was prevalent except in lower- and middle-class homes. In the high-style homes, tile was used exclusively. Wood was used more frequently in lower- and middle-class homes and of a style similar to that used in other parts of the house. However, there is nothing that says you can't use creative and ornate woodwork in your own rendition of a Victorian bath. Utilizing scrolled fretwork in window corners, under shelves and in other unique areas will be fun and will surely convey the message that this is a Victorian design.

Wainscoting was a common feature in period bathrooms and kitchens and is often used in contemporary spaces emulating a period look. This can be a simple wood rail 42 to 48 inches high or paneling with vertical boards below.

BACK TO PRE-INDUSTRIAL CRAFTSMANSHIP— THE ARTS & CRAFTS MOVEMENT

As we moved into the 1900s, the shift in architectural styles from Victorian to Arts and Crafts meant far more subdued and refined moldings and millwork. Bases in the Victorian age with beads and caps became simple, flat and plain, in keeping with the Arts and Crafts ethos.

In custom-constructed houses, handcrafted millwork borrowed from the finest custom design traditions of Stickley and Morris, and incorporated functional joinery including pegged joints, visible mortise-and-tenon joinery and wedges. In millwork's more mass-marketed form, there is little ornamentation and detailing. You will even see Japanese influences, which were popular at the time, in some millwork, even if it was mass marketed.

Arts and Crafts moldings and millwork are characterized by plain faces and square edges. There are few rounded or curvaceous details in Arts and Crafts moldings. Banding with one-by-fours and one-by-sixes

The wainscoting and trim are stained and not painted, as is suggested to be design correct in kitchens and bathrooms of the late nineteenth and early twentieth centuries.

was used powerfully by Frank Lloyd Wright and the Greene brothers in California. It is not as common on lower-style or middle-class homes, most likely because of price issues for the builder.

A hallmark of kitchens in both the Victorian and Arts and Crafts periods is that cabinets often extendeded to the ceiling. This is an important detail to match in the refurbishing or building of a Victorian kitchen on two counts: it provides good storage for bulk items and is historically accurate. It might be noted that because ceilings in Arts and Crafts houses

WHAT MAKES IT VICTORIAN

✳ ✳ ✳ ✳

(above) *In this Arts and Crafts kitchen, other strong period-design details include tile backsplashes and period hardware. Note also the mortise-and-tenon cabinet construction visible about halfway up the side of the cabinet.*

(left) *In creating a period feeling of a true Arts and Crafts kitchen, the owners of this house added many historically accurate elements including unadorned and minimally trimmed-to-the-ceiling cabinetry.*

were often considerably lower than in earlier Victorian structures, even though the cabinetry extended to the ceiling in both styles of architecture, the Arts and Crafts kitchen bears a more horizontal appearance than the vertical look brought about by the much higher ceilings in older houses.

Brent Hull is one of the country's leading experts on historic millwork. Author of the book Historic Millwork: A Guide to Restoring Doors, Windows and Moldings from the Late 19th and Early 20th Centuries, *he is a popular writer and speaker. His firm, Hull Historical, is licensed to reproduce the millwork from Winterthur.*

WINDOWS: THE EYES INTO A VICTORIAN WORLD

Like most elements of architecture and design, stylistic changes usually occur gradually over eras and not weeks. Slowly, from decade to decade and from region to region, changes in roof slope, door size, window shape and architectural footprint take hold. From a left-brain perspective, innovations and advances in manufacturing processes, construction techniques and materials are the impetus for change. From a right-brain perspective, changes can come through an architect's epiphany or an inspired take on an old architectural form.

However, the Victorian period brought rapid and elemental changes to the design of houses and other structures. In part, this was because of technological advances; also, the economics of a nation surged—the middle class swelled. Diversity followed fortune. Fad and fashion took hold. Kit houses were suddenly available; building boomed and one style did not suit everyone. Change and innovation were a constant. Windows—their manufacture and use—followed form as well as invention.

Windows are certainly a highly visible architectural element in any structure and their evolution in size and shape definitely altered the appearance of buildings in the mid- to late nineteenth century. The Industrial Revolution was as much the cause of new window design in the Victorian era as was any other factor.

Prior to the mid-1800s, window sashes were of mortise-and-tenon construction and windowpanes were handblown. Such individually made pieces of glass were usually no larger than 6 x 8 inches framed and separated by wooden mullions. Colonial and Federal windows were typically referred to as six-over-six or twelve-over-twelve—the number of these small panes framed to form a window.

The Industrial Revolution brought mechanized glass-blowing techniques that could make each pane considerably larger. Most post-1860 Victorian houses have tall, double-hung exterior windows high enough for a person to step through. Each window usually consists of only four panes—two up and two down. Given the otherwise highly decorative nature of Victorian design, the simplified look is surprising but typical in most houses of the era.

What gave the Victorian house window its artistic individuality was

(above) *The simple one-over-one double-hung window became part of the architectural landscape of the late nineteenth century. This little kitchen nook couldn't be more inviting.*

(opposite page) *This Indiana bathroom is the epitome of charm and creature comfort. Soft colors, claw-foot tub and lush décor create an ambiance as sensual as ever appeared in any Victorian parlor. The talented homeowner actually painted the curtains on to the wall—they aren't real, but the atmosphere is.*

the incorporation of stained and leaded glass. In that great era of ever-exploding technological and creative advances, there were many stained-glass artists making pieces for the home and church markets.

Windows of all types still play a large role in creating Victorian home design. In today's Victorian house, whether it is a refurbished historic home or new construction, the inclusion of those tall, four-pane, double-hung windows is still iconic to the Victorian look. Stained glass remains a strong decorative accent; its bold colors and shapes in both interior and exterior windows provide drama and a shot of Victorian aesthetic. Since we now want to bring as much design element into the kitchen and bathroom as we do in the other rooms, the inclusion of stained glass makes design sense.

This brings about two basic tenets of Victorian design. If you want

(above) *These highly decorative milk glass arched windows add high style and privacy to this newly created Victorian bathroom in a north Georgia home. In fact, they provide the main design focus in the room. The barrel toilet tank and open shelving add additional Victorian ambiance.*

(right) *The leaded-glass window over the bathtub lets in light and provides an elegant design element in this historic Victorian. The period house belongs to Rich and Jacki Kaiser, of Culpeper, Virginia, who are designers and restorers of stained glass and experts in historic glass.*

to add instant drama and Victorian high style to your kitchen or bathroom, using a piece of stained glass somewhere in that space will give you enormous dramatic bang for your design buck. And if you can possibly find some great piece of antique Victorian glass, there is every chance that it will be of strong artistic merit and well worth whatever you have to pay for it, which will be considerable. Stained and leaded glass are among the best elements of Victorian design that create a unique and rich look.

STAINED & LEADED GLASS
By Rich and Jacki Kaiser

The addition of stained-glass windows and panels to Victorian kitchens and baths is, of course, a matter of personal choice. Whether or not to include them should be based on several factors, not the least of which is historic accuracy. Most Victorian homebuilders, especially those building for the average middle-class family, considered decorative glass as icing on the cake and, due to its cost, put stained glass where it would be most noticed—the front entry, the parlor or the staircase. Kitchens and baths were far down the list as they were the rooms seen least by visitors.

Today's homeowners, however, take pride in their kitchens and bathrooms, which go far beyond the solely utilitarian use the Victorians gave them. This being the case, stained glass has become very popular in both of these rooms.

Kitchens and baths are enhanced by a source of natural light and ventilation. This is as true today as it was in Victorian days. In many cases, these two rooms require a window treatment other than curtains or drapery, and stained or leaded glass neatly fills that need.

The purposes of stained glass were the same then as they are now: to ornament, to obscure an undesirable view or to provide privacy. A stained-glass window in the kitchen might make use of the first two purposes and enhance a view; for instance, a trellis of grapes weaving around a center of clear glass incorporate the garden outside into the window and thereby into the room.

Windows heavy with jewels, bevels and opalescent glass might be appropriate elsewhere, but might overwhelm or darken a kitchen. Often the kitchen included Queen Anne–style windows with colored rectangles bordering a clear center on the upper sash. This was an understated way to bring color and light into a kitchen.

Once again, stained-glass windows provide the main period-design element in the kitchen of this refurbished San Francisco historic house. The colors seem to pierce the rest of the room.

Transoms over doors are an ideal area for ornamental glass, which can be a single pane of special glass or a detailed panel. A transom to the outside can complement the architecture of the home or reflect the character of the kitchen. An interior transom complements the adjoining room; an example is an ornate dining room with stained glass of its own.

Panels in kitchen cabinet doors were, and are, an opportunity to hide unsightly contents, such as canned goods, with opalescent glass in geometric or floral patterns. Beveled or leaded clear glass may also be used to show off fancy place settings and crystal.

The bath had some of the same parameters as the kitchen, with one important addition—the need for privacy. An exterior window, much desired for fresh air, needs to be obscured in some manner—and what better use for decorative glass? Usually, to keep costs down, windows and transoms were fitted with glass of a frosted, glue-chipped or rolled pattern. Occasionally, these types of glass were leaded in geometric patterns such as running diamonds. Again, the Queen Anne style with frosted centers and colorful borders made a bath light and cheerful.

The use of stained glass as a creative option in Victorian kitchens and bathrooms offers myriad choices of unique style and design. The options for adding this lovely art form to home design are endless.

Rich and Jacki Kaiser are husband and wife co-owners of Stained Glass Works in Culpeper, Virginia. They have worked in stained glass since 1969. Rich studied art at the University of California, Sonoma, and has had studios in California, Florida and Virginia. They have done extensive work restoring and creating new Victorian windows for historic homes.

(left) *A long and narrow piece of stained glass in the exterior window of this home provides light and design appeal while also affording privacy.*

(opposite) *The stained glass that is original to this Pennsylvania house is used to great dramatic effect in a downstairs powder room.*

TILE FOR STYLE

Tile has played a huge role in the design of both kitchens and bathrooms of the Victorian era. Following is a brief history of its earliest use, and its manufacture and utilization from the end of the Middle Ages through its stellar reemergence in the Victorian era, and to its current popularity as a decorative and utilitarian building material.

CERAMIC TILE IN THE
NINETEENTH-CENTURY KITCHEN & BATH
By David Malkin

An encaustic tile in its simplest form consisted of an ecclesiastic design made by inlaying one-color clay into colored base clay and firing the tile to bond the clays together. The earliest and most prevalent users of encaustic tiles were monks who made and used them to cover floors and to surround fireplace openings in their monasteries and cathedrals.

Although countless tiles were made for this purpose, following the dissolution of the monasteries by King Henry VIII in the mid-sixteenth century, tile making all but died out. Almost 150 years later, the craft was revived by an enthusiastic potter, Herbert Minton, son of the founder of Minton China who thought that there must be a use for an encaustic tile to repair or restore the floors of cathedrals and abbeys. He was right.

After many unsuccessful attempts in the late 1820s, Minton succeeded in making a viable tile that he introduced in 1843 at a gathering of princes, nobles and bishops in London. As a result, the floors of many cathedrals were restored using the new tile.

Tile has the major design features in this new northern California Victorian house. Homeowners once owned a large late-nineteenth-century house nearby but decided that while they love Victorian, they needed a new house with all the modern bells and whistles to meet their lifestyle. They designed this new kitchen with lots of tile to give it an old-world sensibility.

Then came the Victorian age when Victoria's Prince Albert specified encaustic tiles for Osborne House, which he was building for Queen Victoria. Augustus Welby Pugin specially designed a range of encaustic tiles representing heraldry and other creative and imaginative designs for the floors of the new palace at Westminster. Tile as a building material caught on once again; it wouldn't be long before Herbert Minton's tiles coursed into general use and made their way across the Atlantic. The industry was on a roll and other manufacturers jumped on the bandwagon.

This stimulated the use of ceramic tile for many other purposes, including the hygienic covering for kitchen walls and floors. At first, these were visually utilitarian, consisting of plain white or cream glazed tiles for walls and red, unglazed tiles for floors. Similarly, there were developments in the design of bathtubs, water closets and wash basins for bathrooms, and it followed that tiles should also be used in these newly introduced essentials for the home. Towards the end of the nineteenth century, manufacturers of tile and sanitary ware started the production of decorative effects, which soon became sought-after additions to the more substantial Victorian home. Some of the great English homes of the nineteenth century such as Leighton House and Addison Road in London were tiled with hand-decorated tiles by William de Morgan, who established his own manufactory to produce a Persian-style tile. This became very popular because of its addition of an exotic flavor to Victorian design. Its use, however, was constrained by the costly process involved in its manufacture.

Domestic manufacture of tiles developed throughout the nineteenth century, and ceramic tile in the United States was first produced in the 1870s. During this period, home décor kept pace with design trends. In the Art Nouveau period, tiles were made to reflect that style in bathrooms and kitchens. By the end of the nineteenth century, it was said that no household, institution or public building was complete without them.

CONTEMPORARY TILE USE

During the twentieth century, tiles for all purposes copied the Art Deco period of the 1920s and '30s. Mass production made tiles cheaper and the do-it-yourself age of the 1960s put ceramic tile within the budget of most homeowners. Today, it is possible to produce ceramic tiles in porcelain and exactly copy natural materials such as stone, granite, marble and slate. Tiles in sizes from 4 x 4 inches to 36 x 36 inches can be made without any of the inherent problems of the natural material. Consequently, the use of tile has grown enormously all over the world. Surprisingly, one of the growth areas for design in the last fifteen years has been in what is now called Victorian design.

Whether the real Victorian kitchen or bathroom ever looked like the twenty-first-century idea of Victorian style is a moot point, but the wall and floor tile designs are genuine. If it satisfies a nostalgic feeling for the past, so be it.

David Malkin is an extensively published expert on the history and use of tile. He represents a number of tile manufacturers. All Victorian-style tiles, both genuine and simulated, can be obtained through his firm, Tile Source, Inc.

LET THERE BE LIGHT

Centuries prior to gas lights and electricity, animal fats fueled various forms of ongoing candlepower to shed light on the spaces in which we live. The Victorian era of lighting lies somewhere between whale oil and track lights. Like so many other elements of Victorian design, lighting fixtures of the period were sculptural as well as practical. Today, their use in nineteenth-century-style rooms provides both the light we need as well as the historically appropriate antique aesthetic.

For some reason, those who have expertise in all areas of nineteenth-century antiques sometimes forget about the mood and ambiance of the era. Therefore, one often finds restored Victorian-style parlors ablaze with full and extreme candlepower without so much as a dimmer switch. This lack of aesthetic consideration is also all too often seen in utilitarian rooms such as the period-appropriate kitchen or bathroom.

These are not places that require mood lighting. However, in the true period house, prior to electricity, soft light was produced by the lighting available at the time. Owners of today's period kitchens have the option of adding discreet canned lighting to their period-style fixtures. Some lighting experts and historic purists are all for it and others object strenuously.

Clearly, one must consider how to see what one is doing in those functional spaces, but it is an individual decision. In light of the challenge of satisfying this particular dual purpose of function and form, special attention should be paid to creating the best mix of lighting quality and quantity.

(top) This tin "solar" lamp could be used on a table or hung on the wall. Solar lamps replaced most whale oil lighting because they could burn cheap, clean-burning lard oil made from "prairie whales" (pigs). Lard oil was the dominant lighting fuel in the 1840s and 1850s until it was replaced with kerosene, which was even cheaper.

(bottom) Simple kerosene lamps were in almost every kitchen from 1860 to 1915. Even where gas and electricity were available, kerosene was so inexpensive that it coexisted with other types of lighting. The lamp pictured dates from the early 1860s and is shown with a tin holder that allowed it to be hung on the wall.

Tin lard lamps such as these from the 1850s were the ultimate in efficiency and economy, if not style. Many were designed to heat the font to liquefy solidified cooking grease to provide light that was almost free. There are many American patents for lard lamps, which were widely used through the first half of the Victorian era.

LIGHTING FOR VICTORIAN KITCHENS & BATHS

By Dan Mattausch

The most important thing to remember about historic lighting is that it serves the dual purpose of illumination and decoration. No single object is more prominent or more capable of establishing the atmosphere of a room than the chandelier. It hangs at eye level, in the center of a room, and is frequently big and bright. Despite this, lighting is frequently the last thing considered in a restoration or renovation. Accurate information about lighting is scarce and owners of Victorian homes seeking the example of house museums regularly see inappropriate neo-Colonial imitation candle fixtures or art deco crystal lights in a high-Victorian interior.

An important aspect of using nineteenth-century lighting styles is knowing the dominant lighting technology of a specific period. Renovators interested in decoration may not have a primary interest in whether a lighting fixture used candles or coal gas; nevertheless, a basic understanding of when and where these fuels were used is crucial to getting the style correct.

Those unaccustomed to design vocabulary may find helpful this basic timeline for the dominant nineteenth-century lighting styles and technologies in America.

1830–1839: NEO-CLASSICAL
whale oil and candles

1840–1859: NEO-CLASSICAL AND ROCOCO REVIVAL
lard oil and coal gas

1860–1869: ROCOCO REVIVAL
gas and kerosene

1870–1879: EASTLAKE AND NEO-GREC
(Renaissance revival) gas and kerosene

1880–1889: AESTHETIC (Anglo-Japanese)
gas, kerosene and electricity

1890–1899: BENT BRASS AND PIERCED WORK
gas, kerosene and electricity

While the actual divisions are not nearly as defined as this, and other styles coexisted, this timeline serves well as a simple guideline.

LIGHTING THE KITCHEN

Restorers interested in historically accurate lighting in kitchens are fortunate that here function unquestionably won out in the battle versus form. Kitchen lighting used extremely simple versions of the styles listed above. For example, a sophisticated 1860s parlor may have been lit with a six-arm brass Rococo revival gas fixture that would cost $25,000 today. In contrast, the kitchen in the same house could have used kerosene wall brackets and a single overhead gas light with only a small trace of the Rococo revival style (that would cost only a few hundred dollars now). During the first half of the nineteenth century, and even later in working-class homes, kitchen lighting often included tin fat lamps that could use kitchen grease or lard as a fuel. While these devices look primitive to a modern eye, they were actually quite clever and efficient.

Restoring a kitchen in a style that suggests a Victorian atmosphere, without actually being historically accurate, is a much more common approach. Even in these cases, providing lighting that is appropriate to the style and period of the home allows for a more sensitive and sophisticated approach. Lighting that is totally out of character for a home rarely contributes to a graceful period atmosphere. If a knowledgeable homeowner desires lighting that is more decorative than historical accuracy allows, an elaborate multi-arm fixture that could have been appropriate in another room of the house would have a much better chance of contributing to the desired look of a Victorian kitchen than something totally out of time and place. In other words, try to be true to the period, if not the room.

LIGHTING THE BATHROOM

In terms of historical accuracy, bathrooms are a bit easier than kitchens, since the room could literally be a converted closet (a water closet, or "WC," for those easily offended), or a virtual Roman bath with lighting to match. In an elaborate Victorian bathroom, the light fixture could be comparable in style and cost to those used in a bedroom, with two or even three arms, depending upon the size of the room. On the other hand, a basic water closet might have inexpensive lighting comparable to a small kitchen. In any case, bathrooms were the domains of the family and not the domestic help, so historically there is more leeway for decoration.

FINISHES

In addition to style, the question of appropriate finishes for nineteenth-century lighting is critical. From painted metal to patinated brass, nineteenth-century finishes are wonderfully complex and varied. Although a nickel finish (not as shiny as modern chrome) was very popular in kitchens and baths, it was not universal. By the late nineteenth century, manufacturers frequently offered the same fixture in twenty to thirty different finishes. In addition, the lighting was usually coordinated with plumbing fixtures and door hardware.

The proper finish can have a dramatic impact on the overall appearance of a fixture. Lighting fixtures designed to be faux gilt with painstakingly hand-burnished details that are now black with dirt and oxidation look nothing like they were designed to appear. On the other hand, historic lighting that is simply dirty is still routinely sent to the brass polisher to be stripped and buffed. Fortunately, the importance (and value) of furniture with original paint or stain has been fully recognized. With this in mind, acid dips and hard polishing (i.e., motorized buffing) are procedures guaranteed to destroy the appearance and often the value of early to mid-nineteenth-century lighting.

ILLUMINATION

Once an appropriate fixture has been identified (either a historic piece or a reproduction) and a finish applied, the final questions involve the integration of the fixture with the interior. While making the case for historic lighting levels (especially in house museums), in most instances even a period interior must be well illuminated. The difficulty lies with achieving necessary contemporary light levels while maintaining as much of the historic appearance of the fixture as possible.

Proper electrification of a fixture involves more than sticking a halogen bulb where the gas burner or candle used to be. Approaches that are more creative can result in pleasing effects that do not compromise the integrity of the original design. For example, many candle fixtures can be electrified with concealed bulbs, so real candles remain both prominent and functional.

Sometimes the best solution is to separate the functions of decoration and illumination entirely. Unobtrusive supplemental lighting can highlight a historic fixture, which remains purely as a decorative object. Experience has shown me there is no better conversation starter than a gas fixture that still has its gas burners, especially if they are operational. Efficient lighting can be accomplished with small, recessed, low-voltage halogen lighting in the ceiling or hidden in furnishings, providing for both task lighting and general illumination. While this idealized approach is not practical for every installation, thinking about the crucial role of lighting as decoration early in the renovation process will result in interiors that are far more accurate and pleasing.

Daniel W. Mattausch is an author, lecturer and independent scholar. As a preservation consultant for historic lighting, his recent projects include the White House, the Blair House (the U.S. president's guesthouse), the U.S. Treasury Building, the Library of Congress, numerous National Park Service sites and several major motion pictures. As a U.S. Capitol Historical Society Fellow, he investigated the historic lighting at the Capitol.

This lighting fixture is one of the stronger historic design elements in this refurbished Little Rock, Arkansas, kitchen in a period house.

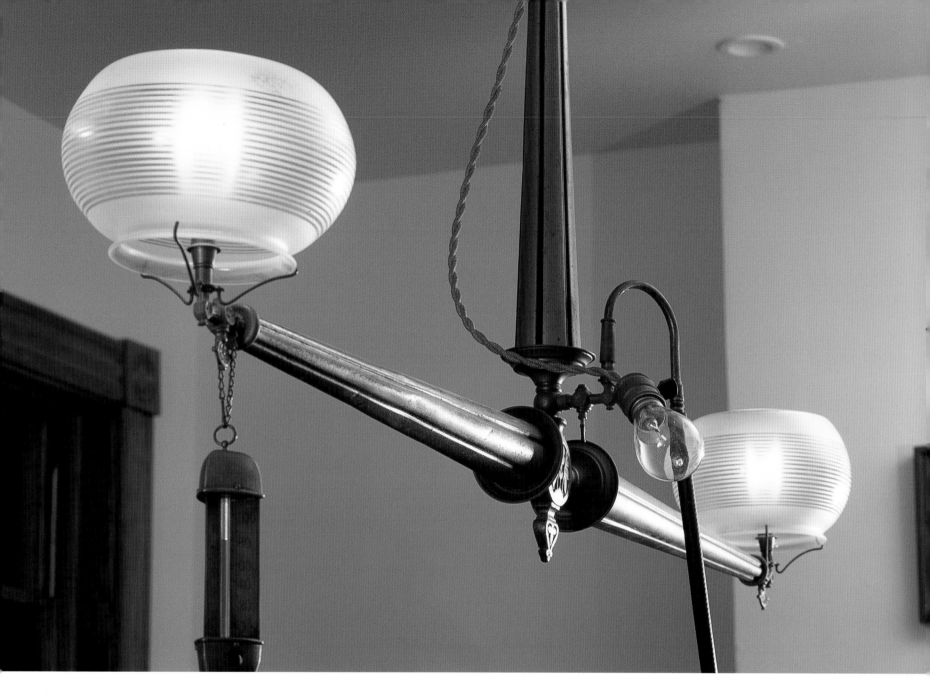

(above) *Gas "T"s, such as this one manufactured by Mitchell, Vance & Co., were popular in utilitarian and kitchen environments from 1870 to 1910. The exposed lightbulb and twisted cloth cord was a practical way to electrify gas fixtures.*

(left) *Simple gas wall brackets (improperly called "sconces" today) were in almost every city kitchen from 1860 to 1910. As technology advanced, the gas burner could be replaced like a lightbulb, but the bracket probably would not be updated as styles changed.*

PANTRIES

Chefs are in. An entire cable television network has made them media darlings. Across America, both men and women confess to being glued to the food channels. No longer are there even home cooks since people now refer to themselves as home chefs. Everyone is buying "professional" stoves, knives, pots and pans. The Victorians had exquisite forks, spoons, picks and knives for every imaginable food; now we have the same number of preparation and cooking utensils. The past is prologue.

"Gourmet kitchen" is now the hinge pin in any realtor's rap. Ambiguous as the term may be, it acknowledges our reborn craving for hearth, home and beautiful space in which we, too, can be the star creators of major feasts.

Like the Victorians, we are enchanted with the exotic, not just in travel destinations, architecture and furnishings but also in the exploration of international menus. Asian, Italian, Eastern European, Latin and African cookbooks are stocked even in small-town bookstores and bend the shelves of people who have taken up cooking. Beyond solely providing how-to recipes, these books are odes to cooking as a lifestyle. One term that keeps coming from the mouths of food-channel chefs and appearing in cookbooks is *pantry item*. This refers to the experts' belief that it is essential to have a full larder of ingredients on hand from around the world.

For the true foodie, it is both practical and comforting to know that at a moment's notice you have the wherewithal to whip up a feast for a dozen in the cuisine vernacular of at least six cultures. Caveman comfort or entertainment chic, the pantry is back as an essential appendage to the kitchen and becomes another space to design and decorate with as much thought as we give to the kitchen.

THE EVOLUTION & REVIVAL OF THE VICTORIAN PANTRY
By Catherine Seiberling Pond

No Victorian kitchen was without its essential, complementary pantry. Since the homes of early America, pantries have existed in numerous forms—and names—for all types of houses. Some were small closets adjacent to a kitchen while others were sprawling areas storing supplies and tableware. Pantries in Victorian homes satisfied the great need for food storage and preparation space. The expansive, meandering nature of Victorian architecture simply allowed for more spacious storage than Federal or Colonial forbears.

Pantries are traditionally cool, unheated and unadorned storage rooms with shelves and cupboards, having access to the kitchen. During the Victorian period especially, pantries provided important additional storage for a generally small but always efficient area for cooking and preparation. It is important to remember the utilitarian nature of the downstairs—or behind-the-scene domestic work area—of the Victorian house. Kitchens were active arenas, generally used only by servants, with limited built-in cupboards or counters, unlike our dream kitchens of today. Therefore, adjacent pantries became useful for providing the kind of storage space a busy kitchen required: perhaps dishes in one pantry and foodstuffs in another, or a combination of the two. In larger homes, pantries were delegated for specific tasks or uses: china, barrels, dry goods, canned goods, a cooler larder for keeping fresh foods, even locked areas for keeping silver.

It was the elaborate multicourse Victorian dinner party with its many dishes and serving pieces that gave rise to the butler's pantry. It was also at this time that specialized silver implements and serving pieces—like pickle forks and jelly spoons—came into more common use. An effective buffer between the kitchen and dining room, the butler's pantry was closeted but of sufficient space where servants could work without bothering the family or their dinner guests. Here the clamor of dishes was kept to a dull roar

(opposite) This pantry in a DeSmet, South Dakota, farmhouse at one of the Laura Ingalls Wilder homesteads is both decorative and practical. It is also timeless and beautiful with its shelf trim and the beauty of the simple cupboard with original paint. This would be a charming corner in any twenty-first-century Victorian kitchen or pantry.

(above) *In this new kitchen in a Virginia period-Victorian house, the pantry is not a separate space but has been sited in an L-shaped corner of the main room. The swinging door leads directly into the dining room.*

(left) *The pantry in the Riordan Mansion in Flagstaff, Arizona, is directly adjacent to the kitchen where the family had easy access to stored foodstuffs as well as extra dishes and serving implements. Today, this arrangement seems to work best in designing a Victorian with a directly attached pantry.*

behind a thick swinging door or screen, hot food was sent up in serving dishes via a dumbwaiter that had likely been sent down in advance of the dinner party (or passed through to the kitchen, if sharing the same floor), and dishes were often washed in a more forgiving copper-bottomed sink.

Meanwhile, shelves, drawers and cupboards stored all manner of china, silver, glassware and serving pieces. The butler's pantry, generally smaller than a china or food pantry, provided everything "at the ready" and was a place for staff to retreat when not required in the dining room. While the kitchen was the cook's arena (the mistress of the house seldom, if ever, ventured there), the butler's pantry belonged to the waitstaff of the household. (Few homes actually had a butler, per se, with most hiring staff specifically for dinner parties.)

WHAT MAKES IT VICTORIAN

✳ ✳ ✴ ✳ ✳

ON THE FARM

The nineteenth-century farmhouse had its architectural evolution from about 1850 to 1910 and is as significant in the history of the pantry as its urban and suburban counterparts. Here it was more common to eat and gather in the kitchen while reserving the dining room for special occasions. The farm wife and perhaps one hired girl (and certainly able daughters) prepared the meals as well as most of the staples that a family ate. The Victorian farmhouse pantry was a veritable grocery store: what they didn't grow or raise on the farm, they got only on occasion from town. Therefore, ample space for dry goods was essential. Butter- and cheese-making equipment, vegetable and meat storage, dry and baked goods, and special items all had their own spaces, always adjacent to the kitchen and either within the house or an adjoining shed. (Kitchens and their pantries were generally in the ells of nineteenth-century farmhouses.)

Farm kitchens generally had one or two pantries: a buttery, or butt'ry (not named for butter, but for the "butts" of storage barrels), or larder—both more archaic terms for *pantry*—and generally a milk room where butter and cheese were made, stored and kept cool by a spring-fed water source. Technology would eventually enable the self-sufficient farm wife to do her own canning and freezing—other kinds of long-term provisions that required additional storage.

Pantries were almost always found in suburban homes built between the end of the Civil War and the 1920s, yet they would become smaller and more streamlined. Homes during these periods retained their small, utilitarian kitchens, and a butler's pantry often connected the kitchen and dining room. The Victorian legacy of separating workspace from family living was prevalent until the post-war house. Even then, the kitchen was often removed from living or play areas. By the mid-twentieth century, kitchen pantries had become the size of utility closets where canned goods shared cramped space with mops and brooms.

TODAY'S PANTRY

Pantries remain a vital part of today's kitchen. With fully outfitted gourmet kitchens and a preference for buying foods in bulk, we should not be surprised that pantries are in demand in houses both new and restored. Homeowners fortunate enough to have an actual Victorian home are often sensitive to these pantry areas and continue to utilize them in their modern kitchens. We have emerged from tiny post-war kitchens with small storage closets to grand, public cooking spaces central to hearth and home.

Today's pantries—as their Victorian originals—play an important role in this realm of food and dish storage. We don't shop every day as our mothers and grandmothers often did; in this era of nesting, we like to stock up on supplies for any reason. No longer necessarily behind a shut door, pantries are often functional but attractive display places for all manner of kitchen collections. There is a comforting security in knowing the twenty-first-century larder is full. Today's pantries are both a practical and nostalgic nod to their Victorian originals—a must for any kitchen, large or small. ❋

Catherine Seiberling Pond has a master's degree in historic preservation and has written for major design magazines, including Old-House Interiors *and* Victoria. *She worked for several historic house museums—including the Gibson House Museum in Boston, Massachusetts.*

This is the pantry in the Victorian farmhouse at the Laura Ingalls Wilder Homestead in DeSmet, South Dakota. Here you would find far fewer dishes, eating and serving implements. This space would have been used to keep store-bought supplies such as flour and sugar, home-canned foods and homegrown produce.

Borrowing Décor from the Parlor

✷✷✷✷✷✷✷✷✷✷✷✷✷✷✷✷✷✷✷✷✷✷✷✷✷✷✷✷✷✷✷✷✷✷✷

Period Kitchen Redo

Doing a Victorian kitchen or bathroom in an old house amid the constraints of protecting its historic integrity and design is challenging. It can be far more problematic than creating Victorian-style kitchens and bathrooms in new construction where the homeowner can call all the shots on layout and décor. For those who have fulfilled their dream of owning a period home, the purchase of which may have involved years of planning and saving, the following section offers advice from those who have been there.

TO REMODEL OR REINVENT: RESTORING A PERIOD KITCHEN

By Robert Esposito

Twenty years ago I bought my crumbling 1870s Italianate villa in the historic district of Williamsport, Pennsylvania. Like most preservationists faced with restoration or remodeling, I had no hesitation telling the electrical contractor to install a virtual labyrinth of wires and cables to every room. But when it came to the original kitchen I stopped dead in my tracks! What was I going to do with the kitchen? And what was I going to do with the bath? YIKES!

It was then that I thought of a friend of mine, Howard. He wanted me to see his "new" old home and in particular the kitchen he had just restored. His mother had offered to pay for the work needed in the kitchen as a house-warming gift. So, he set about finding the correct historic materials, having cabinets custom made; he carefully oversaw the colors, renovated a period stove and even hid the refrigerator in the basement to make everything as authentic as possible. When all was complete, he brought his mother over to see the results of his labors (and her bank account). As she looked around, taking in all the details, she turned to him and said, "Now Howard, it's all very nice, but I hope you realize you've just spent a great deal of time and money on a kitchen that now looks very much like it needs to be remodeled!"

This new/old kitchen in a northern California home has all the elements of a period kitchen. Its greatest feature, however, is the inviting homely atmosphere that today's designers and homeowners seek.

(right) *A great look for any vintage or historic bathroom is to set a basin right into a washstand. It was done then and the look is just as attractive now.*

(opposite page) *The homeowners utilized a bold wallpaper border like one that could be found in the parlor or any public room in the house.*

LEARNING FROM HOWARD

That remark is probably true of many rooms that preservationists restore, but not the thing most historic homeowners want to hear. So how can we, as keepers of the flame, historic homeowners, preservationists or simply people who appreciate the graciousness of the Victorian era, reconcile ourselves to the presence of side-by-side refrigerators the size of garages, microwave ovens with digital displays, electric pasta makers and Jacuzzis in our old house?

The truth is that if the Victorians had had such myriad modern marvels available, they would have used them too. What Victorian, even during the patriotic zeal of the centennial in 1876 or Colonial revival in 1900, would choose to brick the floor of their "new" kitchen and install a huge hearth where they could spend the rest of their days tending to fires and basting roast beasts on spits they would crank endlessly by hand? They

would have locked up such an individual. So today, how can we go about retaining a historic or nostalgic feeling in our kitchens or baths without worrying that our family will have us institutionalized?

Over a century ago, a revolution occurred in Victorian design led by Charles Eastlake and his patron, the Prince of Wales. More than style, Eastlake espoused a philosophy of living that most of us today take for granted. He suggested that life should become less formal, more natural. Toward that end, he specifically suggested that people should have "living" spaces rather than "withdrawing" spaces in their homes. Wanting to be in fashion, the Victorian drawing room gave way to the living room, a term that we still use. As our lives have become less structured and formal, gradually more of our homes are comprised of spaces for enjoying the activities of daily life with those around us. The kitchen, no longer just a place where food is stored and prepared, has become the heart of our homes, the

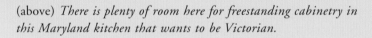

(above) *There is plenty of room here for freestanding cabinetry in this Maryland kitchen that wants to be Victorian.*

(left) *This kitchen, with gracious roominess, is the perfect place to put a freestanding cabinet for display of collectibles or storage. Pieces like this can often be found at a good price because they don't easily fit into contemporary rooms.*

place where family and friends gather and are entertained while preparing and enjoying a meal. In essence, the kitchen of today has become another living room. Its decoration can now reflect more warmth and hospitality than the highly varnished walls and zinc-covered counters that our Victorian past provided.

Too many options can lead to confusion. As you probably know, both the kitchen and the bath are easily the most expensive rooms to design and furnish in terms of cost per square foot. Thought and planning should start this process. You might consider soliciting the advice of a professional with experience in such matters. Such an individual can help you think along avenues you might not have considered. A minor investment in some basic consultation can be invaluable over the next few decades of living in a well-planned kitchen or bath.

The importance of finding a contractor or architect with a proven record of sympathy for the special quirks and idiosyncrasies of an old house cannot be stressed enough. Check that the people you hire are interested in doing the sort of work you want and that their craftsmanship is what you expect.

CASING THE JOINT

Cabinets are often the single most expensive cost in the kitchen (unless you plan to install a twelve-arm black Venetian glass chandelier over the breakfast table). Often, the easiest place to find some ideas can be your local corporate monolith of construction materials. However, I have repeatedly found that local cabinetmakers can provide significantly better quality products for surprisingly less cost. What they provide will not only be specific to your own space and needs but will also be unique to your home. Much of what you are paying for in a cabinet or piece of furniture, or even a car for that matter, will not be seen. The quality of materials directly relates to the longevity of the cabinet, so make sure you know what you are paying for. Here are some questions to consider:

- Are the cabinet backs and sides made of particleboard or plywood?
- What are the shelves made of?
- Are veneers being used as opposed to solid wood?
- How thick is the veneer?
- Are these veneers actually wood or plastic laminate?
- Can the hinges stand up to a stiff breeze?
- Does a micro-thin layer of veneer hide some manner of ingenious and semi-worthless substitute for quality building materials?

Most Victorian kitchen cabinets were quite simple with squared, recessed-panel doors. They were also often painted and almost never ran in one continuous length from wall to wall around the entire room. These simple design elements are your best choices when selecting from the myriad cabinet and door styles available. Such choices will also be good for the budget.

I also suggest that you follow an idea taken from your parlor or living room. Examine the furniture in these other rooms. Note that the doors and drawers of your better furniture usually fit flat within the framework of the cabinet and do not flop on the surface to cover a smaller opening. Cabinets constructed like pieces of furniture are not available in as great a number as their simpler counterparts, but you may be astonished at the amazing difference this will make in your kitchen's final appearance.

If your kitchen space is large enough, nothing says that you can't place freestanding cabinets in strategic places around the room without having to fill every available inch of space. A baker's rack, desk, or even a comfortable settee for guests can fill any available voids. If your ceilings are high, there is no reason your new cabinets should not be taller than usual. You can always use the additional storage space. Finally, don't be afraid to think outside the box, or cabinet, as the case may be. Above high windows I have had cabinets constructed with frosted-glass backs and glass doors to serve as both display and a light source in the kitchen. Be creative!

I SEE THE LIGHT

Even if your budget is modest, try not to save by buying inexpensive light fixtures. There are some beautiful reproduction fixtures available today. (Even the plainest hand looks good with a big diamond on it!) Typically, the Victorian kitchen would have had a single modest central light source, often a plain two-arm gas fixture. These, however, even if electrified with high-wattage bulbs, may not provide adequate lighting to all work areas. With our current technological innovations, it is a simple matter to inexpensively augment light by hiding it above or below the cabinets. (See the chapter on lighting by Dan Mattausch, page 89).

FINISHING UP

The finish on the cabinets as well as the walls will also determine how much light the kitchen receives. Wooden wainscoting was often installed with countless layers of paint and varnish for durability and ease of cleaning. Walls were often finished in a like manner or occasionally tiled. Decorative faux finishes can provide a departure from the monotony of plain painted walls, or several very nice reproduction wall coverings are available to provide the illusion of tile. More adventurous homeowners might consider applying an appropriately patterned reproduction tin ceiling to their walls, making certain to paint in a hypothetical grout line between the hypothetical tiles. However, among my pet peeves is the use of reproduction tin ceilings in residential applications. Tin ceilings were almost always used in commercial applications during the Victorian period. Nothing makes a home look more like a store to me than seeing a tin ceiling installed in a kitchen, however meticulously.

ARE YOU FLOORED BY IT ALL?

Floors can present a particular problem in a new "old" kitchen. Though reproduction linoleum is once again available, reproduction floor cloth is much more difficult and expensive to acquire. If you have a desire for some-thing gaudy and can find something that approximates tile at the same time, then go for it. Perhaps the new styles of linoleum can be less taxing and acceptable. For those with bigger budgets there is an endless array of tile available, but usually the tile that looks most appropriate is only meant to be used on walls and would not stand up to foot traffic. Without appropriate options available, make a selection that will remain innocuous within the context of the completed project.

COUNTERTOPS

With the incredible array of different building materials available for use as countertops today, I can only suggest you take a Valium and be prepared for an overwhelming shopping experience. For those without budget constraints and who like sumptuous color, there are blue granites available that must be dragged out of the African jungle by elephant. Please don't get too crazy with your countertops. Trying to make that blue granite merge quietly into harmonious concert with the rest of your kitchen could be like trying to make a factory whistle sound good at the Boston Pops. Granites, marbles, faux marbles, butcher block, tile, laminate, limestone, and concrete all can have their place. If you have a particular interest in pastry- or candy-making, then don't forget a slab of marble somewhere. Perhaps this might be a good time to call that design consultant?

AND ANOTHER THING

The island below a pot rack is not a new concept in kitchen design. If you have the space, then feel free to use one just as your Victorian fore-bears would have—even though theirs might have been nothing more than a simple farm table. Besides offering more work area, it also allows you to face your family and friends. The island helps you to better utilize the floor space available while preserving the existing door and window openings. My own kitchen has four walls but five doors and two windows! Without an island, I'd have to cook outside.

There's an obvious requirement in this kitchen in Marshall, Texas, for a major pot rack. Although contemporary, the rack has been decorated to fit in with the homeowner's Victorian tastes.

(this page, left) *All elements except the commode, tub and sink are borrowed from the parlor in this dollhouse depiction of a high-style Victorian bathroom.*

(this page, right) *This bathroom, with galley-like dimensions, incorporates the accents necessary to give the sense that one has gone back to another century.*

(opposite page) *Light, bright, airy, white and wicker are all the words you need to describe this delightfully inviting bathroom in a Victorian farmhouse near Madison, Virginia. As wonderful as it is, it wouldn't be that difficult to emulate.*

BATHROOMS

Today, with all that is available in the restoration marketplace, it is relatively easy to re-create whatever type of bathroom might be appropriate to the age of your home, down to the toilet-paper holder. Many of the suggestions I offered about the kitchen can also help in decorating the bathroom. As the bathroom was not the place for servants, it was more likely to be decorated to resemble the other rooms in the house. Depending on how authentic one chooses to be, one could include a wicker chair and a light similar to those in the hall or bedroom. A simple rug and something framed could be hung on the wall. There is a real temptation among twenty-first-century historic homeowners to be carried away in littering their bathroom with bric-a-brac. I would suggest you overcome that temptation.

Our current level of knowledge and technology allows us to be less obsessed with sanitation and hygiene than were our Victorian counterparts. So it is possible to make the bathroom a much more comfortable, warm and well-decorated environment. Unfortunately, if you wish to be somewhat authentic you will probably have to employ a measure of restraint. Where you might indulge yourself is in the selection of ornate hardware and linens.

It is encouraging that more people are interested in acquiring an older home and have concern for what might be historically appropriate when they redesign and redecorate its interior. Never has more information or material been available to aid in the process. Whatever you do in your old home, it should bring the same pleasure and joys as it did for its previous owners. Please think about how you will pass it on to the next owners who will be its caretakers.

Robert Esposito is an art and architectural historian, designer, decorator, consultant and antiques dealer who has been helping people preserve and restore their historic homes and gardens for the past twenty years. He specializes in the nineteenth century in America.

BORROWING DÉCOR FROM THE PARLOR

COLOR & PATTERN

A major icon of Victorian style is color. A bold and voluptuous mixture of vibrant peacock jeweled tones and patterns, singular or in multiples, typify Victorian décor. Pattern-on-pattern wallpapers and solid paint tones interspersed with borders of yet other patterns cover the walls and ceilings of grand parlors of Victorian houses. Public rooms were—and are—all about drama, and even though the kitchens of those multipatterned parlors were probably whitewashed plaster, we can now take that spectacular ball and run with it, pushing the color envelope right into our contemporary Victorian kitchens and bathrooms.

Contrary to popular thought, even among those who are students of early design, the Victorians did not invent the use of strong wall color. In early Colonial and Federal houses, walls were painted bold reds, dark greens and mustards—all highlighted by gleaming white-painted trim. Over years, as these houses were refurbished, often the color had faded, giving the restorers the idea that the original tones had been muted.

Whether or not strong colors originated with the Victorians or their ancestors is less the issue in decorating a Victorian-style kitchen or bathroom than which colors work best in each of those settings. And because color plays such a major role in Victorian style, you need to consider carefully how and where you are going to use it in designing a kitchen that borrows decorating elements from the parlor.

WHICH, WHERE

Among the issues that should be deciding factors in choosing wall and ceiling tones is one's own personal color comfort level. Don't choose bold colors and patterns for any room unless you are comfortable living with them. Take a cue from the rest of the rooms in your house: if your other rooms have walls of quiet pastels, it probably means these are the shades that best suit your personal aesthetic. Don't choose

(above) *The owner of this house was not afraid to use a pattern in giving a modest-sized bathroom life and interest.*

(opposite page) *Victorian-style tub, sink and wainscotting on walls create a feeling of the Old World in a new house.*

What a sensual room. Other than the wallpaper that marries so gently with the curtain material, notice the terrific idea the homeowner, Ann Tobias, had in adhering a period-style mirror frame onto a wall-to-wall mirror. Her ceiling tones are flawless with the wall treatment, giving a total warm ambiance to the space.

bright tones for the kitchen or bathroom just because you feel they are correct for the style and period. You can find other Victorian-appropriate design icons such as stained glass, stained trim and moldings to express your nineteenth-century style.

However, if you can establish that a bright and strong color is comfortable in a room you and your family will probably spend at least as much time in as any other, it's time to start looking at which tones will look good in your kitchen. Yellows reflect light well and can give the room a sunshine-like glow; reds are rich and warm; blue is a cool tone and some

decorators suggest refraining from blue walls in a room where food is either prepared or eaten. Their reasoning is that blue tones reflecting on food alter its visual attractiveness. If you love blue, who cares?

PATTERN

As for pattern, consider that the kitchen probably has more elements in it than other rooms of the house. Appliances and hanging pots and pans might fight boldly patterned wallpaper. If you really want to borrow from the parlor in your own rendition of a Victorian kitchen style, consider wainscoting below and papering above. This would cut the amount of pattern while still welcoming it. Another idea is to use solid color and add a dramatic wallpaper border from the ceiling a few inches down on the wall. Both borders and stencils are means to achieving some visual Victorian pizzazz without overwhelming the room; they can actually provide two-fold design benefits in seemingly opposite architectural situations. They can either bring your eye up in a room with tall ceilings or add a color and style statement to a room with only eight-foot ceilings.

Color and pattern can also be picked up in fabrics of window treatments. Even a simplified Victorian swag across the top of the window adds nineteenth-century softening and romance and provides some tone to the room.

Among the designs typical of the Victorian era are patterns of flora and fauna. Animal prints were also in vogue. Late-nineteenth-century Victorians were enamored of nature and introduced materials that expressed this passion into their décor at every chance. If you don't know much about historic textiles, either consult a decorator or talk to a knowledgeable salesperson in a fabric store. She or he will direct you to the fabric sample books of companies that make copies of period-accurate textiles, so your décor will be period authentic. There are also companies making fabrics expressing their own rendition of things Victorian, if you just want the Victorian attitude and sensibility without the authenticity.

Since we are not going back to the Victorian era and nobody is testing for historic authenticity, pick colors and patterns you love with the abandon of a Victorian and you will always enjoy being in the rooms you design.

(above) *The wallpaper in this kitchen, with its modest, lighthearted design, adds a light and warm backdrop to simple cabinetry and furnishings.*

(top right) *You have to like people who love purple. What more can we say?*

(bottom right) *This charming bathroom corner has a way with white. Here, the homeowner thought—and rightly so—that just one color accent, on the tub, was enough.*

(above) *Obviously, this kitchen with its high ceilings, transom glass and original wainscoting is in a Victorian house. The timeless, vintage effect of the wallpaper blends in cleanly and appropriately with the architectural elements.*

(opposite) *Against a backdrop of simple subway tile, the floral-patterned textiles lend an aura of elegance to this space. Given that, the formal fixture doesn't seem out of place at all. Sometimes a small space is easier and more fun to decorate than a larger one.*

HOW TO DESIGN A KITCHEN THAT LOOKS HISTORIC, NOT DATED

By Patricia Poore

You know those Victorian-style kitchens that have become popular in the past decade—the ones with furniture-quality cherry cabinets, bright brass hardware and lighting, English tile backsplash, polychrome tin ceiling, and reproduction wallpaper? Beautiful as they are, these are not authentic period kitchens; rather, they belong to today's Victorian revival.

Unless you're a curator, you probably don't want an authentic Victorian kitchen. But you may not want the anachronism and expense of a parlor-quality revival kitchen, either. What to do? Consider creating a rather simple kitchen made with timeless materials and incorporating some elements from elsewhere in the house, such as trim, molding or window details. Or, "date" your kitchen to a slightly later time period—say, 1900 to 1925.

RESTORATION OR REVISION?

Kitchens in old houses rarely escape remodeling. Most of the time a remodeled kitchen is the first thing a new owner wants to tear out, because it already looks dated and is probably inferior in design to the rest of the house.

To avoid putting in a kitchen that will shout "2005" ten years from now, take cues from the house rather than from the kitchen showroom. A kitchen inspired by the house's design details and its historic period will always fit. Such a kitchen is timeless, and thus less likely to look dated in the future.

If there is anything left of the original kitchen, do not rush to demolish. Something historic or usable—or even a clue you can use when you build—may be lurking in the room. Take the time to discover if there is anything that can be salvaged from the old kitchen such as the general floor plan, a separate pantry, the flooring or a base cabinet. (Of course, if you have inherited a true period kitchen—good design and craftsmanship from an earlier time, even if it postdates the building of the house—that's a rare find, and very cool, and you should keep it.)

How far you want to take period details is a matter of preference and budget. Consider designing a simple, functionally modern kitchen, but one that includes materials or details from the rest of the house. This is a very popular approach for old-house owners and can result in rooms that range from quite plain to the fancy revival kitchen. Generally, keeping it simple gets you in less trouble. The "interpreted" period kitchen is more believable if details come from the pantry, not the high-Victorian parlor (and it's cheaper too).

Another approach among old-house nuts is the scenario kitchen. You make up a story about the history of the house. (Sometimes, it's even true.) For example, let's say you're working on an 1880s Queen Anne. The horrible 1960s kitchen you inherited has been gutted and you're starting with an empty room. But, you don't want the kitchen to look new. So, you build a few cabinets that look as though they are original, with 1880s

Everywhere you look in this Peru, Indiana, kitchen there are architectural artifacts that work together to create an inviting room. Pity the homeowner who didn't save or salvage such wonderful things when they had the chance. Homeowners used and incorporated all historic elements to their best advantage.

(this page) *Behind-the-scenes utilitarian functions in this kitchen are evident. (They even have a secret handcrafted door in a hallway that their cats can push open to get to their litter box.)*

(opposite page) *The Lexington, Virginia, family wanted a Victorian house with all the bells and whistles of new construction. So they built their dream kitchen with cabinetry that elicits the handcrafted charm of Victoriana without being dated to any specific decade.*

What a wonderful area. This Dallas, Texas, homeowner incorporated a Victorian architectural artifact, vintage store display, sundry containers, dishware and serving pieces, and lovely tile to create a timeless historic effect. The cost was low, the imagination was high.

construction details that match pantry cabinets you measured in an intact house. Then imagine that a well-heeled previous owner renovated the house circa 1925, when electricity went in and so did the stove (which you have just bought as an antique). You'll build features of your new "old" kitchen around those two dates, even going to the trouble (or fun) of collecting late-1920s and early '30s dishes and utensils.

With this "story of the kitchen" approach, you get modern (not Victorian) function and at the same time a period feel. Somehow, vintage 1900 or 1930 (or even 1950) looks less dated than a really contemporary kitchen—because the older styles are already historic, and you have hindsight on your side in picking the best of whatever period. If you were to look at a 1980s magazine layout of decorator kitchens, you'd see that they already look dated. By using period details, you'll naturally pick only the materials and design that had staying power.

A period-inspired kitchen will *not* ruin your resale value (as long as you do have a dishwasher, refrigerator, decent stove and storage). In the past few years, people seem to want exactly those things found in very old-fashioned kitchens. Pantries are back. So are freestanding ranges, drain boards and unfitted furniture. The period kitchen today has more in common with current homeowner desires than does any kitchen fad since the 1930s.

Although this is a kitchen in a Victorian home, the wallpaper, some of the decorative accent pieces, appliances and other elements come from a later period. But, because of the architectural aspects and the historic nature of the room, this kitchen is historically appealing.

GUIDELINES

So what are the rules for designing a timeless kitchen in an old house? A list of dos and don'ts follows. Read them for their general wisdom. Any rule can be broken, of course, as long as its spirit is understood and your reasons are considered.

- DO keep it simple. In the kitchen, you don't need relief tiles in the backsplash, a border around the floor, a custom hood, a wallpaper frieze, art glass, carved brackets, cast brass hardware and a Victorian-style ceiling fan—more to the point, you don't need ALL of those in the kitchen.

- DO rely on timeless materials such as wood and stone. Downplay contemporary materials by keeping design simple or incorporating period conventions—trimming out laminate counters in wood, for example, or using honed rather than polished granite.

- DO base design on something real. That might mean echoing your dining room's panel construction or moldings in your new kitchen cabinets, or if your neighbors have a house of the same period, consider taking cues from their kitchen or intact butler's pantry.

- DO use conventions, colors and materials that were in use during the period. If kitchen floors were pine, use pine. If stoves were black and sinks white, there's your color palette answer.

- DO look to original sources rather than taking off from later interpretations. For example, go for historical reproductions of fabrics from the period, rather than buying "traditional" fabric that is a textile company's 1970s idea of Victorian.

- DO use nickel (or, for kitchens after the 1920s, chrome). Fancy brass plumbing fixtures and lighting generally don't belong in a Victorian kitchen.

- DON'T use recessed lighting. Just don't.

- DON'T let too many showroom ideas creep in: this year's colors, the tile mural over the professional range, the gargantuan refrigerator, the recycling center or the vast island complete with plumbing.

- DON'T worry too much. If you've read this far, you're probably the sort that will get it right, whatever your taste and budget.

BACK TO BASICS

Surviving Victorian kitchens in museum houses suggest a few conventions. Softwood plank flooring, about three inches wide, was most common in Victorian kitchens. Walls were often covered with bead board, either floor to ceiling or as a wainscot low on the wall with plaster above. Plain tile was used in some urban kitchens, especially around the sink and stove. Bead board was shellacked, or stained and varnished; later, it was often painted with a semigloss or gloss enamel. Walls were most often painted an off-white or yellow: cream, bisque, beige, light tan, pinkish beige, maize—but not bright white.

Although not common in kitchens, wallpaper more likely would be found in modest houses where the family entered the kitchen, not in the servant kitchens of the wealthy. Plain roller shades in light tan or dark green were common on the windows; muslin curtains and lace panels were also used. Furniture was freestanding and counters minimal and shallower than today's 24-inch standard depth.

A great benefit of period-inspired design, besides making your kitchen timeless, is that it limits your choices to a reasonable number. We can all use that kind of help.

Patricia Poore is owner and editor-in-chief of the magazine Old-House Interiors, *and the former owner and editor of* Old-House Journal. *Her work on old houses goes back to the 1970s; she restored both a Brooklyn row house and a shingled English Arts and Crafts cottage near the sea in Gloucester, Massachusetts, where she lives with her two sons.*

While everything in this kitchen makes it a functional work area, one can't really tell if it was updated in the 1920s or 1990s.

The drawer pulls and fretwork are indications of the Victorian period. The key to this room, however, is in its simplicity and functionality, the very definition of a historic Victorian kitchen.

(above) *This kitchen was actually built in the early twentieth century. It hasn't changed much; the patina of the woodwork has only gotten better over a century. However, that doesn't mean it can't be replicated.*

(right) *What could be more timeless than this original stone hearth in northern Maryland? The wood throughout supports the antique environment that could have been created at any point from the last 250 years through yesterday.*

(above) *This kitchen shows the space as an interesting place to spend some time. There's no reason to relegate all art and collectibles to the living room.*

(left) *This is another view of this kitchen near Boston, Massachusetts. The family enjoyed collecting an extensive array of period objects. They were proud of the fact that their efforts added the perfect touches to their Victorian farmhouse.*

ART, ANTIQUES & COLLECTIBLES

It is probably unnecessary to reiterate that we are now decorating our kitchens and bathrooms in a way that our Victorian ancestors did not. Since family time now means kitchen time, décor in that room is now a consideration that it wasn't in those years. However, even our predecessors thoroughly enjoyed visiting their bathrooms, which historians tell us were sometimes sensually high style. Now both rooms have become lush grounds for the inveterate collector of art and objects, which is the aesthetic soul of the Victorian taken a hundred plus years down the road.

In early prairie and farm kitchens of the mid- to late nineteenth century—the height of the Victorian era—one might have found stern-faced family members glowering from early formal black-and-white or sepia-toned photographs hung on whitewashed kitchen walls. This was the beginning and end of the art found in most Victorian kitchens. The pictures probably hung in those kitchens because that room also served as both dining and living room.

In the kitchens of period formal Victorian houses—city and suburban—there was almost no ornamentation. But even in true historically rendered houses of today, we borrow from the Victorian design and art aesthetic to make kitchens visually pleasing.

There are several ways to go in using art and collections in a Victorian-style kitchen. If one chooses, one can stick closely to the Victorian's simple design spirit of those early rooms by using as artwork some of the objects that were then thought of as solely utilitarian.

USEFUL DOESN'T MEAN UGLY

Hand-woven baskets for storing and carrying produce, hand-forged iron cooking implements and utensils, and farrier-crafted lanterns are just some of the items that were then food storage and preparation essentials that have become highly sought after, prized and often costly antique collectibles. These objects of great beauty in form and style probably went unnoticed by whoever was using them to prepare meals. Today, they have been elevated from objects of function to works of handcrafted art. We view them and other cooking accoutrements, such as copper and iron pots and pans, trivets, choppers and spatulas, with an entirely different eye. Artfully arranged on today's historically styled kitchen walls or on shelves, they become decorative pieces that are entirely appropriate for even the greatest historic purist's style palette.

In the kitchen, other such items, once solely work tools—now displayed in collections—are a new form of art collectible. Washboards, sad irons, eggbeaters, rolling pins and even potato mashers are grist for this art mill. If we look at them as if we have never seen them before, and are unaware of their mundane usage, we now recognize their sculptural forms. As any collector of anything will tell you, two is a pair, three is a collection. In arranging a collection of small objects, before hanging them on any wall, try placing them on the floor or large table in a creatively graphic arrangement.

GRANITEWARE

Continuing in the same vein of using as art those objects that were not originally designated as such, graniteware needs to be singled out as one great design statement. These metal cooking utensils of every sort—from pots and pans to strainers, colanders, tea and coffee pots, plates, cups, and bowls—were hugely popular in Victorian kitchens of the mid to late years. Their popularity, use and manufacture continue today—most often as reproduction and to hoodwink the antiques collector.

This Mississippi antiquer thoroughly enjoyed assembling this fascinating assortment of antique and vintage pieces, and creating the most attractive corner in her period farmhouse.

This antique pie rack, sitting under a collection of rolling pins, is great for storing useful collectibles. One or two vignettes like this can create a feeling for an entire room.

(opposite page) Overdone, you say? Not so for this North Carolina collector of Victorian-era graniteware who took his collecting passion to the nth degree. He started buying up those pieces when they were relatively inexpensive. Over time, the stuff has skyrocketed in price and popularity. While you may not want to cook in his Victorian farmhouse kitchen, you can't help but enjoy his treasures. Having fun in your own home with your own stuff is important.

Yelloware, whether on cupboard shelves or on a tabletop, is intrinsically Victorian kitchenware. Shelf pieces—less than perfect, with worn chips or extensive crackling—can be had for just a few dollars. These items can function in their original uses or become part of the artwork of the kitchen.

It's remarkable how a small, inexpensive assemblage of vintage items, when grouped together, can add life to a relatively quiet room. The cabinetry, while of a period design, is clearly contemporary, but a sense of Victoriana is obvious.

(opposite page) A period-Victorian step-back cupboard just off the kitchen is a great place for this Indiana homeowner to put some of her treasures. The warm wood surrounds her collectibles, which, when grouped together, make them much more attractive than they would be standing alone.

Although graniteware was made in every primary color and pattern imaginable, blue and white was the most-produced color combination and is the color most often found in antiques shops. Popular both in the United States and in Western Europe, where they were also made and used, designs were spattered, swirled, marbleized and created in myriad other patterns. They were usually in a strong color against a white background, but sometimes multicolored.

Appreciation of these objects has been consistent with their price; it has skyrocketed. Compared to other art objects, however, graniteware remains relatively affordable and brings life and color—and no small amount of authenticity—to kitchens.

HANGING AROUND WITH PAINTINGS

In the same decorative style, we can reasonably hang paintings on Victorian-styled kitchen and bathroom walls. However, even with all the technological advances in appliances, food preparation creates grease and bathing can cause steam to rise. Therefore, which kinds of art to exhibit should be a consideration. Also, even in the most formally designed house, the kitchen and bath are likely to be casually furnished and used. While tastes in art are entirely subjective, art objects—even those of the Victorian era—of a lighter mood and spirit would be most appropriate to the spirit of the room.

Artists of the era painted tableaus of fruit and produce and seemingly endless renditions of kittens. Charming and perhaps a bit overly sentimental farm scenes were popular topics. These subjects point to the Victorian's love of, and rediscovery of, nature. Hanging art of this type is entirely design appropriate for a Victorian-style kitchen. And the same can be said of the bath.

This farmhouse detail expresses not only the homeowners' passion for things Victorian, but also how easy it really is to make even a kitchen corner an artful, welcoming place. Notice how the family isn't afraid to mix old photographs with other two-dimensional objects.

SIGNS OF THE TIMES

Other great favorite art objects entirely suited for kitchens are the beautifully designed advertising signs, especially antique, handmade ones. Hung alone or in graphic groupings, they bring a kitchen to life and become an accepted art form in both the decorating and art worlds. While never, of course, seen in early kitchens, advertising and shop signs create the ambiance of the period. They can be extraordinarily designed and cost more than all your appliances put together, or they can be of a more common variety and still add a colorful dimension. Reproductions of these signs, particularly the ones embossed in metal, are found everywhere. Often, however, these repros are obvious as such and can cheapen an otherwise well-designed room.

If graniteware and advertising memorabilia seem a bit casual or less than artful, consider arrangements of silver and toile-painted trays, and porcelain platters and bowls on walls and on plate shelves hung above windows. These, too, bring form, color and design in a slightly more formal and traditional way.

IS IT ALL A CROCK?

Of course, the artful antiques that are so highly prized among collectors are crocks. Fired throughout American history, these decorative pieces, ranging from the diminutive to the five-gallon size and bigger, reached a peak of usefulness during the Victorian era as storage containers. They are often ascribed to individual makers or locations. The decorative blue under the glaze, as well as the maker and, of course, condition, specifies rarity and price. Their value continues to ascend and can range from the low hundreds to well into five figures. This is not an antique collection that should be entered into innocently or lightly, but it can add quite a strong statement to your kitchen décor and will certainly be period pure.

PACKAGING THE PERIOD

At the other end of the cost spectrum, and easily available, are tins that held all products available to the consumer in the nineteenth century. They come in a variety of shapes, and the imprinted designs can be ornate and decorative. In small or large groupings, they can be very effective ornamentation. Original period packages can also add a decorative touch.

VICTORIAN ANTIQUES

In many kitchens designed to look Victorian, you will find collections of seventeenth- and eighteenth-century china hanging on walls and Windsor chairs pulled up to Sheridan-style country tables. One might say that is not true period décor, but in fact, it is. The Victorians used early objects as art and décor just as we do today. What was antique to them, heirlooms passed down from family members or purchased, is also antique to us. The use of cross-generational objects is perfectly within the scope of Victorian design in kitchens, bathrooms or any other room of the house.

Human culture has become a bit more egalitarian and sophisticated than it was in Victorian times. Most of us don't rely on servants, whose comforts Victorians usually didn't even bother to consider. Most of us in the twenty-first century don't blush in horror at the mention of bodily functions. Still, some things haven't changed: the craving for beauty is as alive in today's families as it was 150 years ago.

Love of art objects—and lots of them—is one of the glorious tenets of Victorian design. Clutter isn't a must in any Victorian room but it certainly is as at home today in kitchens and bathrooms as it was in early Victorian parlors. There are as few limits in incorporating art and artifacts today as there were to the voracious collecting appetites of the Victorians.❋

(above) *Useful dishware that is also attractive need not be hidden behind closed cabinets. It is also more to the period to have open shelving.*

(opposite page) *This Victorian kitchen on the coast of Maine is not only well used by its owner when he entertains, but also is a place where he and his guests enjoy his extensive collection of stoneware. Blue and white is still the favorite palette of choice for collectors and homeowners.*

(opposite page) *This kitchen in Williamsport, Pennsylvania—a town where there is no end to Victorian architecture—favors the blue-and-white combination of décor. Simplicity and space allow for attractive groupings of collections.*

(above) *With a divergent arrangement of various period artifacts, this kitchen, even without the fireplace, high ceilings, transom glass and other architectural aspects, could be nothing but Victorian.*

(opposite page) *Bathrooms can also be wonderfully enjoyable places to arrange one's collections. Victorian themes are easily and inexpensively implemented in such confined areas as shown in this bathroom in the mountains of Georgia. Remember, there are no rule books.*

(above) *This bathroom reflects the style and taste of the adjoining bedroom. A japanned cupboard stores wonderful period antiques. This picture could well have been taken more than a hundred years ago (but it wasn't).*

BORROWING DÉCOR FROM THE PARLOR

This could either be new construction or a remodel of a period house. Here, in this kitchen on the coast of Maine, the homeowners chose to incorporate enough of the new to make it a highly functioning kitchen while retaining the Victorian sensibilities of décor and architectural design. Indeed a happy marriage.

Contemporary Victorian

✻ ✻

The New Victorian

If you are taking a contemporarily designed, essentially new Victorian-style house and designing a kitchen and bathrooms, you have more latitude than if you are trying to be true to the design of a historic home. However, there are still design challenges. While it is relatively simple to create a Victorian atmosphere in living rooms and bedrooms, the kitchen and bathroom may be a bit more problematic in their décor.

It is always a balancing act. Do we opt for only period atmosphere or accommodate visual acceptance of twenty-first-century life? How much do we draw from each and how do we evoke nineteenth-century ambiance in new constructions?

New homes are not necessarily environments for inhabitants with Victorian souls; one doesn't preclude the other. Without getting lost in a time warp, there are simple and comfortable ways to enjoy Victorian ambiance in contemporary structures.

START NEW, THINK OLD: KITCHENS & BATHS WITH SOUL
By Erika Kotite

One of the strange rituals my older sister practiced in the late days of summer in the 1970s was Levi's bashing. She and her friends bought brand-new jeans, which they proceeded to wash with lots of bleach, slap over and over on the concrete patio and pick at the seams and hems so they would prematurely fray. By the time school began, she and her friends would be clothed appropriately in soft, "time-worn" jeans that looked just right.

The appeal of jeans that are old before their time applies to many elements of our aesthetic lives. Everything, from garden urns and window treatments to interior paint and bedcoverings, seems to benefit from a bit of antiquing. We all know from watching the *Antiques Roadshow* that whatever you do, you don't try to refinish or deep clean an antique desk (can you pronounce *patina*?). The elements working their changes on the piece over time have become an important part of it. Time is the only master of this art; we who want our surroundings instantly patina-rich must settle for clever selection and good taste to find adequate substitutes.

With structural entities, the challenges of making new appear old become larger. You must get the details right, but even achieving perfection in the details won't disguise any glaring modernity that lurks beneath. The right stain can make fir look like oak or walnut, but it cannot make today's standard-size cabinetry look Victorian. Moldings provide height and depth to walls and cabinetry, but if they are sized too small or too large for the object they are placed upon, then they are an expensive failure to meet the goal of looking authentic.

(left) *This is a new kitchen in an old Victorian house. According to designer of historic properties Dudley Brown, "An unusual color dictates that of the woodwork." His research revealed that this historic color name is "tobacco." All of the interior trim in the original service wing of the mansion was of tone and Dudley incorporated it in the new kitchen. Great care was given to trim the interior with molding profiles and panel configurations that exactly replicate those of the house.*

(opposite) *This is a newly created kitchen in a period house in Culpeper, Virginia. Utilizing wallpaper, window height and cabinetry suggesting the era, the homeowners made all the right design moves to create a Victorian world. Every part works with the others so that it doesn't matter when it was built.*

Paradoxically, the quest for "period authenticity" in a new kitchen or bathroom starts with successful set design. Set designers draw on iconic elements to create a completely imaginary world, yet one that allows the audience to feel genuinely transported to that particular place and time. We must be our own set designers and draw upon the expertise of professionals who really understand and appreciate Victorian design to get the look we want. A new house with the right bones—high ceilings, natural wood floors, turned and detailed millwork—is the appropriate stage for creating rooms that look and feel old, even if you can still smell the fresh-cut wood.

The most important elements for any kitchen are the cabinetry and the appliances. Most late-nineteenth- and early-twentieth-century designs strive for the unstudied look of freestanding furniture (a compilation of cabinets, tables, shelves and closets), with varying heights and door sizes. If space allows, then the kitchen must have an island, and a well-equipped one at that. Today's islands wear their names well, providing enough prep space, storage and cooking areas to be "parakitchens" in their own right. And, despite its air of modern innovation, the island aptly reflects the all-important kitchen table of the past, where maids or wives had most (if not all) of their workspace for chopping, slicing and dicing.

The effort of maintaining order and culinary integrity gave

(opposite page) *The owners of this old house designed and built a farm-house kitchen juxtaposing the main part of the house. The Victorian-era accessories, furnishings and wooden island countertop add the timeless attitude the room required.*

(above) *It takes so little to do so much. A period-style Victorian slipper tub and fixture, a flowerpot from Provence, tile to wainscot height and softly colored walls, and you have a romantic Victorian enclave. All this is at La Campagnette, an inn situated in Boyce, Virginia. Does it matter that this bathroom was only recently refurbished?*

145
✳ ✳ ✳ ✳

kitchens a humble appeal. Not much has changed in the basic principles of appliances—ranges, ovens, dishwashers and refrigerators are still rather plain, hardworking inventions that have cut our cooking efforts to a fraction of what they were a hundred years ago. Today's vintage-inspired kitchen is served best with unobtrusive gas ranges, stainless or wood hoods, or an antique or reproduction stove. Wood-paneled refrigerators and cabinets hiding microwaves and coffeemakers allow the eye to dwell on the aesthetics of the room.

Just as they spent as little time as possible in the kitchen, the Victorians had very little need to spend time in a bathroom—except for in its most basic role. Bathing, hair-washing and styling, grooming, and applying makeup occurred infrequently or in another room or area of the home (faces were usually washed at a small commode in the bedroom, for example). Small, dark and tucked away in an upstairs hallway, the early bathrooms in fact weren't even considered rooms—just water closets.

Fast forward to the twenty-first century, and when it comes to bathrooms, bigger is truly better. In historic houses, a homeowner usually has to convert an adjoining bedroom into a large master bath. In new construction, bathrooms are designed as large as 200 square feet. Modern tastes and habits call for bathrooms with spa-size tubs and roomy showers, double sinks and changing space, and a toilet area that can be closed off.

And yet in a contrary sort of way, these new oversized bathrooms lend themselves very well to the substantial materials and fixtures of the past. Try fitting a full-size claw-foot tub into a 1960s tract home; it's quite a challenge. The same holds true for lavatories made from modified antique cabinets, large pedestal sinks, high-tank toilets and sturdy chrome holders for bath towels and fluffy terry-cloth robes. These are the elements that bring comfort and period style to a bathroom, no matter how old the house really is.

Large or small, the Victorian-style bathroom is just that: a style. We look to the past for inspiration as well as the natural materials and the craftsmanship to create our bathrooms—and there is a terrific variety of fixtures and furnishings on the market to make this all-important space just right—while leaving the less desirable detractions of the past behind.

None of us really wants a 1900 house, without electricity, refrigeration, running water or adequate storage. Today's dream kitchen is all about space and convenience, a place to prep, cook, nosh and wash with ease. Our bathrooms have evolved far beyond the realm of the water closet; they are much more about living and relaxing than ever before. Take advantage of a new, clean canvas on which to draw your old-world dreams. Then take the time to make them come to life.

Erika Kotite, editor of Victorian Homes Magazine, *is a nationally recognized expert on the Victorian era, a longtime member of the Jane Austen Society of North America and a member of the board of the Victorian Society.*

A hideaway place is what a bathroom could also be about. The structural stage was set for this getaway in its high ceiling and expansive window.

FLIGHTS OF FANCY

We all know that the Victorians were utterly fascinated with exotic travel and incorporated elements of design from other cultures into their homes. They were most taken with the East—China, Japan and Turkey. Furniture was "japanned," that is, painted and embossed in Asian style. Vast collections of imported china appeared in dining room cabinets, and Turkish smoking corners were the rage in Victorian parlors or as separate rooms. Travel was proof positive of wealth and sophistication: wealth to go abroad and bring home objects from exotic destinations, and sophistication to cleverly incorporate them into one's décor. This era was the genesis of show and tell.

With that spirit intact, some people now choose to translate the look into a more contemporary style and take off on flights of fancy in their kitchen and bathroom design. Unbound by any history-specific restrictions, these rooms still maintain Victorian high style. Instinct, it seems, has the best answers and often makes the best decisions. If rooms could smile—here they would.

These contemporary Victorians adopt the color, pattern, romance and eclecticism at the heart of even the most historically pure Victorian rooms and are cloned to their spirit. Would a time-traveled Victorian from 1889 recognize these rooms as being of their style? Perhaps some would not; but probably more would. We do.

One can have fun with the boldness of Victorian color and ride with a passion for the ambiance of the era while including both contemporary and international design elements. One need not be hampered by the confines of historic Victorian design. Homeowners who go with their imagination and a sense of abandon in the face of empirical parameters offer us inspiration to take chances and enjoy living in our own style of Victoriana.

The epergne-like piece on the counter, stained glass and hearth-like stove hood add contemporary drama in Victorian style.

KITCHEN CONSERVATORY

By Bruce Johnson

The original kitchen in our circa-1900 house was, typical of the era, in the basement. Obviously, we wanted a kitchen in the main part of the house (because although we would like to have had them, cooks and scullery maids didn't come with the property). We also wanted a conservatory—a light, bright and airy garden room that would visually incorporate our patio. Not having either, we decided to build both kitchen and conservatory as one.

In designing the kitchen, we incorporated elements of Victorian décor that were in keeping with the rest of the house while allowing for the contemporary and functional. Since we entertain a lot, comfort and convenience in food preparation were also primary considerations. Fortunately, there was a butler's pantry just off the dining room that we were able to maintain in its original location, adjacent to the new kitchen. We replaced its dumbwaiter that led to the basement with floor-to-ceiling storage cabinets that matched those that were in the kitchen. We were also able to place our refrigerator in this location, disguising it behind matching cabinet panels. This united new and old construction and added functionality to our addition.

Among the Victorian design elements we used in the creation of this room were the decorative mosaic tile floor, a hearth-like appearance of the stove that we placed against the wall, and large griffins adorning the tops of the cabinets to make them look more like freestanding furniture than commercial cabinets.

To incorporate the conservatory feeling, we used large floor-to-ceiling windows on two full walls that open onto a patio, so a light-flooded space opens up. The tile floor that is so kitchen-appropriate is also authentic for a conservatory of the era. Only when you step into the room do you realize that this is the kitchen.

By no means did we ever mean to design a true period-Victorian kitchen, but we have borrowed from and distilled the baronial feeling that was pure Victorian and therefore we feel that we have kept to the intent of the era and gone beyond.

Bruce Johnson is a Washington, D.C.—based builder and designer. He has refurbished major Victorian houses in the area.

(above) *Bruce Johnson explains that this butler's pantry was "just off the dining room that we were able to maintain in its original location." This room "united new and old construction and added functionality to our addition."*

(opposite page) *Bruce Johnson used his decorator and construction talents to create an unusually appealing room reflecting his love of Victoriana.*

(left) *If Victorians had the technical abilities that we have today, surely a well-traveled person of that era would have created just this kind of bathroom. The space is pure Victorian in its blended grandeur and sensuality. Considering the arches, the tiled floor, the generous proportions and the subdued palette, why would anyone want to finish their routine and leave this room?*

(opposite page) *This corner of Bruce Johnson's upstairs bathroom in Washington, D.C., is a new room created in an old house. It includes a sink cabinet that is perfectly appropriate to the overall décor.*

(left) *The Johnson kitchen countertop plays well against his fine oil painting and the Victorian architectural elements leading into the butler's pantry.*

(opposite page) *A silver tray on a countertop in the butler's pantry highlights the backsplash tile. Decorative elements bring even a pantry to life.*

MY HONEY OF A KITCHEN

By Marcia Miele

PLANNING

I thought long and hard about what I wanted in a kitchen, which was a remake of space in our period Victorian house, and I was afraid I might be embarrassed if it didn't turn out well. I wanted a place where my guests could hang out and be comfortable. Because I am not the most organized cook, I am usually finishing something when my guests arrive and they always end up in the kitchen. This space had to be roomy enough to accommodate quite a few people and since our family cooks together, it had to be laid out so the guests would not be in the way of the cooks. Finally, the work area had to be large enough to accommodate everyone who is pitching in.

I wanted a warm and inviting environment, sort of an antidote to the sleek and glossy kitchens that are in a lot of magazines. Aesthetics are as important to me as efficiency. The room had to be beautiful since our family and friends would be spending a lot of time there.

My father was born in Italy and I love all things Italian. I seem to have a genetic affinity for tile and marble. My brother-in-law rented a villa outside of Rome and our family cooked his birthday dinner there. The kitchen was amenable to a lot of cooks. The counters and back-splash were tile and there was a long marble table in the middle of the room. There was a fireplace at counter height. We all cooked and sang and had a great time. That kitchen inspired our kitchen.

The color scheme was inspired by a platter I found in Porto Fino that was covered with golden lemons, reddish purple grapes and turquoise leaves on a deep blue background. I took the plate to the tile store to try to match the rich colors.

Finally, all of these requirements needed to fit into our circa-1890

Rob Esposito, Marcia Miele's friend and designer, describes her kitchen as "Venetian palazzo meets Queen Anne." This space is a remarkable culmination of talent, ingenuity and creative acumen using knowledge of Victorian design and architecture.

Victorian house and look appropriate. The original kitchen was long gone and had been replaced with an apartment kitchen. The only original elements left were an old butler's pantry and a back staircase. We kept both and worked them into our design plan, using the butler's pantry to determine the scale and design of the other cabinets.

TILE

The centerpiece of the kitchen is a tile painting behind the stove. I had a brochure from a tile store in Sicily. Our local tile store tried to find a source for the Sicilian tiles but was unsuccessful. They said they could find someone local to paint a design if I had a picture. We chose a peacock picture with a decorative floral leaf pattern in the background because the peacock and floral design could fit into a Victorian scheme. The painter personalized the painting by including a honeybee because my last name is Miele, which means honey in Italian.

COUNTERTOPS

For counter surfaces, I chose marble and butcher block, both surfaces that would have been used in Victorian homes. The marble is a rich-looking rojo. The marble cutter advised me against this choice, suggesting granite. The marble has spotted and is not altogether glossy anymore but it still looks beautiful and I tell myself that I do not want it to look pristine anyway.

ISLAND

We decided on an island design so that guests could be in the kitchen but be separated from the cooks. The surface is butcher block. The island is large in keeping with the large scale of the rest of the room. At first, the butcher block looked like this huge expanse of wood—almost too big, and then it started to get dirty wherever we put things on it. Our contractor, who can figure out anything, found a

surface sealer that was used in the early 1900s that was food safe and could be easily cleaned. I decided to try tiles on the area next to the oven where we put hot pans, and tiles on the other end of the island to balance the look. We also put tiles around the sink to avoid mold. The effect is stunning, but one tile has cracked so we are still not sure if it is a practical solution.

CABINETRY & WOODWORK

For the woodwork and cabinetry, we used elements from the original butler's pantry, the existing woodwork in the house, and a carved wooden headboard. Bob Esposito, our designer and close friend, had found an antique headboard earlier and thought we should try to use it somewhere in the house. We both agreed that the carved floral piece could be used to frame the tile backsplash behind the stove. Our contractor framed the area with molding that matched patterns elsewhere in the house. The result, combined with the tile painting, is spectacular.

We noticed that on the original kitchen door, the inside of the door was different from the side that faced the hall. The hall side was solid cherry with a glossy finish while the kitchen side was a combination of less expensive woods so that the door had several different colors and grains of wood. We carried that motif through in the cabinets that have two-toned walnut and cherry stains. The contractor used design elements from the door and the butler's pantry so that the cabinets have a connection to the old woodwork.

The scale of the cabinets is huge as the butler's pantry cabinets reached to the 10-1/2-foot ceiling. The casings and moldings are very similar to those in the rest of the house. They are not quite as elaborate, but the kitchen would have been less ornate than the rest of the house anyway. We used bead board to cover the under-counter appliances because this material is a nineteenth-century treatment.

Marcia thought tile around the sink would balance the tile on the rest of the island and help avoid mold; while she loves the effect, she's not sure if it's practical. Practical or not, it looks great.

FIREPLACE

The kitchen in Italy had a fireplace that we could cook on and I very much wanted to cook on ours. However, the idea turned out to be too expensive because we would have needed a lot of chimney work. We compromised on a gas unit that is black cast iron, which Victorians might have used. The unit is counter height, which makes it quite visible. It provides a lot of warmth and is aesthetically pleasing and practical. We have lost some of the romance by being able to just turn it on, but it is convenient and we use it all the time.

FLOORING

There was some original pecan flooring that we wanted to save but only enough for a small area. I liked terra-cotta for the remainder of the main kitchen floor because the color looked good with the rojo marble on the countertops. For our sunporch/breakfast room I wanted some kind of slate. I was looking at slate tiles wishing I could find something to complement the slate outside on the patio. We explored the idea of a random pattern of irregularly shaped slates. The effect is almost like creek stone. It is not what I had envisioned, but I love it. The one item that Bob Elion, my partner in life and in the kitchen planning, insisted upon was radiant heat underneath the floors. It has turned out to be a wonderful idea, especially since we have cold stone floors. We can now enjoy being in our sock feet all winter.

APPLIANCES

I originally wanted one of those beautiful French Godin stoves. I justified the price by telling myself that I drove an old car so I should be able to spend car-like money on my stove. But the ovens in the French stoves were very small and in the end I realized that I could get all of the appliances for about half the price of the stove. I had been cooking and entertaining for years on an apartment-size stove, so basic, good appliances would be a great improvement. I settled on a Jenn-Air stovetop because it had four burners and a grilling unit. I also decided on two ovens, which, as it turns out, we use a lot.

While a dining area adjacent to or in a kitchen mainly existed in Victorian farmhouses or came into being in the early twentieth century, it has become the standard in today's home, Victorian or contemporary. Marcia's space also suits the added function of being an attached sunroom.

SUNPORCH/BREAKFAST ROOM

Our old porch had been converted into an apartment kitchen. We decided to keep it enclosed but with windows and three doors that would open and make it seem porch-like. We removed the wall-covering and exposed the original brick and the original porch ceiling that was bead board with wooden beams. We even kept the original paint color on the beams. The three doors needed to open up to something, but a deck would not have suited the house.

We considered a covered porch with a gabled roof that would follow the lines and include the wooden details of the other porches. I wanted the sun to come in during the winter months; this would not have happened with a covered roof. We decided on the framework for a gabled roof without the actual roof. We copied the balusters and gable ends of the other back porch. Wisteria is growing over the framework so the area will be shaded in the summer but not in the winter. We find ourselves spending a lot of time in this sunroom and on the porch.

The fireplace is reminiscent of early Victorian kitchens and creates the kind of ambiance that instantly makes an essentially utilitarian room a comfort zone.

UPSTAIRS BATH

We wanted a bathroom that two people could use, with two sinks. Our contractor suggested the curved wall to make more room for closet space in the room behind it. We also decided on a curved shower stall and rounded sink base to relate to the curved wall. My brother-in-law, who's also a woodworker extraordinaire, made the paneled cabinetry for the rounded sink base and the tub.

The wallpaper scheme that makes the room look almost decadent was put together and applied by Bob Esposito. No one else would have had the patience or the ability to make the cuts that it took to cover the curved wall and ceiling with elaborate patterns. The wallpapers are from the Bradbury & Bradbury Victorian collection. The light fixtures are also Victorian-era reproductions. I chose marble and tile again not only because I love them but also because they could have been used in this house originally.

I live in this lovely old house with Bob and our nine-year-old son, Dante, who is quite particular and spends a lot of time thinking about how we should decorate. Fixing our house is a lifelong process for us. Repairs and renovations are challenging and often expensive, but we have the sense that the house is worth the effort and that we're doing the right thing.

Marcia Miele is co-owner of the Peter Herdic House in Williamsport, Pennsylvania, offering fine dining in a restored Italian villa–style mansion. Her family has recently purchased the Victorian house next door, the Peter Herdic Inn, offering overnight accommodations.

(above) *Stained glass is beautiful, of impactful design and affords privacy. In this space, it was used to bring in light from a porch behind the bathroom.*

(opposite page) *Homeowner Marcia Miele and her designer, Rob Esposito, came up with so many ideas in the creation of this unique Victorian bathroom. Some of these ideas are just pure great design and some are Victorian specific. The division of the space affords dual use. This is enormously practical in old houses where, unlike newly built houses, there are usually fewer bathrooms. Note the Victorian-style pedestal sink and faux marble-painted wall.*

(this page) *Another piece of high-style Victoriana is this japanned cupboard in the Miele bath. It's a highly effective design, but simple to do; Marcia picked up the colors of the cabinet in her window treatments.*

(opposite page) *On the other side of the Miele divided bathroom is the bathing area. The jewel-tone design is lush and inviting. The master bedroom is behind the adjoining door. Note the unique curved wall.*

(above) *In Ann Tobias and husband Ray Hertz's Texas kitchen, bold color makes the Victorian statement. Strong red walls and cabinet tones coupled with a historic-feeling red-and-white toile are two relatively simple elements that, in combination with Ann's collection of period blue-and-white china, create a kitchen that certainly is suggestive of Victorian design spirit in a brand-new house.*

(left) *Good Victorian design lies in the details. The tile backsplash, copper accessories and a natural stone countertop are all elements that add up to a historic late-nineteenth-century feeling. Another period-suggestive element is the hearth-shaped enclosure for the stove fan above the cooktop.*

MY FABULOUS KITCHEN & BATH

By Ann Tobias

It all started with a love of flow-blue china and an antique shop in upstate New York with hundreds of blue and white dishes—love at first sight—all shapes, sizes and patterns—all affordable!

They were instant art to me, and I put them on walls, on shelves and on the table. These dishes dictated the style and the color of my dream kitchen. Five hundred wallpaper books later, I found I also loved toile—especially a red Schumacher toile that looked so homey and inviting that I've used it in my last three kitchens. The finishing touch was a furniture finish of red to match the wallpaper and disguise the cabinetry—to coax it into looking like furniture instead of kitchen storage.

This finish of seven or eight coats of various oil paints and varnishes makes anything wood look warm, inviting and elegant. I used it in all cabinetry, carvings and anaglyphic paper to refine and tie together the five little rooms that make up my kitchen—butler's pantry, utility room, breakfast room, bar and actual kitchen area. Violetta granite-top counters with flecks of deep red and German antique glass-front cabinets to display the flow blue complete the look.

Even though I've never cooked a meal in my life and probably never will, my kitchen looks like the friendliest room in the house. The spirits of hot apple pie, roast chicken and laughing company permeate my all-American Victorian kitchen.

I love toile so much I also used it in my powder room and guest bath.

My bathrooms are furnished with Victorian antique furniture and accessories, as every other room in the house is. I make no distinction between a bathroom and any other room when it comes to decorating.

In Victorian spirit, paintings, chandeliers, silver teapots and lace curtains are all included in the bathrooms to give them the same style and interest as the rest of the house. Faux-finish furniture painting also changes ordinary bathroom cabinets into real furniture with texture and interest.

Ann Tobias is a Dallas-based designer of women's fine evening wear. She is also an opera singer.

With the exception of bathroom necessities, one would never know that Ann Tobias' bathrooms were rooms of that nature. She has pulled out all the stops on Victorian elements, making the décor in her bathrooms blend perfectly with the rest of her Victorian house.

CONTEMPORARY VICTORIAN

(this page) *Yet another example of Ann's use of Victorian design elements in her bathrooms is the antique Eastlake mirror mounted over her master bathroom sink. This mirror would fit just as well in a hall or bedroom. It is among the elements that define this room as Victorian.*

(opposite page) *This is an example of out-of-the-box Victorian design. Ann used cord and tassels one might find on throw pillows or on window treatments to provide a faux separation between the toilet nook and the rest of the bathroom. It doesn't exactly provide privacy, but it does contribute a large piece of high late-nineteenth-century style to the small room.*

RESOURCES

The following is not a complete listing of every service and purveyor of appropriate products for creating or re-creating a Victorian kitchen and/or bath. There are reputable people and businesses—hundreds of them—that can furnish excellent products or services. Such listings are available on the Internet and in many design-specific catalogs. Therefore, we wouldn't even try to list them here.

Instead, this resource list is a unique compilation of those individuals and businesses about whom we have personal knowledge, whose work we have seen, or who have been recommended to us by people whose opinions we respect. Many of the following people and organizations are not listed in major compendia of sources or Internet compilations. They are from our own private list of the best in their field.

As we are in the unique position of discovering the finest experts and organizations involved in Victorian design, décor and renovation, we will be passing additional names on to our readers through the creation of an interactive medium.

We have also had the opportunity to get to know people who share the same grand passion for all things Victorian. The following new Web site will allow readers of this book to access new information and resources and communicate with each other and us over matters that are of mutual interest:

www.VictorianKitchensAndBaths.com

We look forward to seeing you there.

PHOTOGRAPHY

Franklin & Esther Schmidt
F & E Schmidt Photography
feschmidt@earthlink.net
www.FESchmidtPhotography.com

p. 20: top two images courtesy of Thomas Crapper and Company, Ltd. Bottom image courtesy of www.vintageplumbing.com

p. 34-35: images courtesy of www.antiqueappliances.com

p. 48: top left images courtesy of Thomas Crapper and Company, Ltd. Bottom two images courtesy of www.vintageplumbing.com

p. 49: image courtesy of www.antiqueappliances.com

p. 86: images courtesy of Tile Source, Inc.

CABINET MAKERS & MILLWORK

Hull Historical Millworks, Inc.
201 Lipscomb Street
Ft. Worth, TX 76104
817.332.1495
www.hullhistorical.com

Mill's Pride
423 Hopewell Road
Waverly, OH 45690
800.441.0337
www.millspride.com

Plain & Fancy Custom Cabinetry
Oak Street & Route 501
Schaefferstown, PA 17088
800.447.9006
www.plainfancycabinetry.com

Wood-Mode, Inc.
One Second Street
Kreamer, PA 17833
877.635.7500
www.wood-mode.com

Kitchen Cabinet Manufacturers Association
1899 Preston White Drive
Reston, VA 20191
703.264.1690
www.kcma.org

FIREPLACES & WOOD STOVES

CFM Specialty Home Products
   Vermont Castings
   Majestic Fireplaces
410 Admiral Boulevard
Mississauga, ON L5T 2N6
Canada
905.670.7777
www.myownfireplace.com

FLOORING & CEILINGS

Resource site:
www.flooringguide.com

HISTORIC INTERIOR DESIGN

Robert Esposito
415.515.7235

Victoria Imperioli
SVE Designs
917.748.6099

Jean Dunbar
Historic Design, Inc.
108 West Preston Street
Lexington, VA 24450
540.463.3291
dunbar@rockbridge.net

Bob Kane
570.322.2692

C. Dudley Brown
Preservation, Restoration & Interior Design
710 E Street, SE
Washington, D.C. 20003
202.546.7176
www.cdudleybrownassociates.com

Larkin Mayo & Gary Yuschalk
Victorian Interiors
www.lebold-mansion.com

HISTORIC DESIGNERS & BUILDERS

Bruce Johnson
Dupont Erections
202.797.8721

Ken Wittman
691 Woodland Avenue
Williamsport, PA 17701
570.327.1527
www.wittman-spins.com

HISTORIC MUSEUM HOUSES

Laura Ingalls Wilder Memorial Society, Inc.
P.O. Box 426
DeSmet, SD 57231
800.880.3383, ext. 2
www.liwms.com

Tinker Swiss Cottage
411 Kent Street
Rockford, IL 61102
815.964.2424
www.tinkercottage.com

Farmington House Museum
3033 Bardstown Road
Louisville, KY 40205
502.452.9920
www.historicfarmington.org

Cameron-Stanford House
Oakland, CA
510.444.1876

Riordan Mansion State Historic Park
409 Riordan Road
Flagstaff, AZ 86001
928.779.4395
www.azstateparks.com

Alexander Ramsey House
265 South Exchange Street
St. Paul, MN 55102
651.296.8760
www.mnhs.org

HOSPITALITY INDUSTRY

(Bed & Breakfasts, Inns, Restaurants)

Adelphi Hotel
365 Broadway
Saratoga Springs, NY 12866
518.587.4688
www.adelphihotel.com

L'Auberge Provencale
P.O. Box 190
White Post, VA 22663
800.638.1702
www.laubergeprovencale.com

Villa La Campagnette
P.O. Box 190
White Post, VA 22663
800.638.1702
www.laubergeprovencale.com

The Conyers House Country Inn & Stable
3131 Slate Mills Road
Sperryville, VA 22740
540.987.8025
www.conyershouse.com

Morrison-Clark Historic Inn & Restaurant
Massachusetts Avenue & 11th Street, NW
Washington, D.C. 20001
800.332.7898
202.898.1200
www.morrisonclark.com

Richmond Hill Inn
87 Richmond Hill Drive
Asheville, NC 28806
888.742.4536
www.richmondhillinn.com

Wellscroft Lodge
P.O. Box 7
Upper Jay, NY 12987
518.946.2547
www.wellscroftlodge.com

The Peter Herdic Inn
411 West Fourth Street
Williamsport, PA 17701
570.326.0411
www.herdichouse.com

KITCHEN & BATHROOM
(Plumbing Appliances & Fixtures)

Thomas Crapper & Co. Ltd.
The Stable Yard
Alscot Park
Stratford-on-Avon
Warwickshire CV37 8BL
England
44 (0) 1789-450 522
wc@thomas-crapper.com
www.thomas-crapper.com

Thomas Crapper & Co. Ltd.
U.S. distributor:
DEA Bathroom Machineries
495 Main Street
Murphys, CA 95247
209.728.2031
www.deabath.com

KITCHENWARE & FURNISHINGS

Le Creuset of America
877.273.8738
www.lecreuset.com

Plow & Hearth
800.494.7544
www.plowhearth.com

LARGE APPLIANCES

Resource Web site specializing in
vintage-appearing appliances:
www.appliance411.com

Antique appliance restorations:

AntiqueAppliances.com
30 West Savannah Street
P.O. Box 389
Clayton, GA 30525
706.782.3132
www.antiqueappliances.com

Don Hooper
www.vintageplumbing.com

Kohler Plumbing

444 Highland Drive

Kohler, WI 53044

800.456.4537

www.kohler.com

Waterworks

800.927.2120

www.waterworks.com

LIGHTING

Rejuvenation

2550 NW Nicolai Street

Portland, OR 97210

888.401.1900

www.rejuvenation.com

Daniel W. Mattausch

    Dan@gaslights.org

     www.gaslights.org

Fellow, The United States Capitol Historical Society

200 Maryland Avenue, NE

Washington, D.C. 20002

800.887.9318

www.uschs.org

RUGS

Claire Murray

P.O. Box 390

Ascutney, VT 05030

800.252.4733

STAINED GLASS

Stained Glassworks

Culpeper, VA

540.825.0438

TEXTILES

Waverly

800.423.5881

www.waverly.com

Brunschwig & Fils

75 Virginia Road

North White Plains, NY 10603

914.684.5800

www.brunschwig.com

TILE

Tile Source, Inc.

David Malkin

4 Indigo Run Drive, #4021

Hilton Head Island, SC 29926

843.689.9151

www.tile-source.com

WALL COVERINGS

Bradbury & Bradbury Art Wallpapers

P.O. Box 155

Benicia, CA 94510

707.746.1900

www.bradbury.com

WINDOWS & DOORS

Andersen Corporation
100 Fourth Avenue North
Bayport, MN 55003
651.264.5150
www.andersenwindows.com

Allyn Historic Sash Company
P.O. Box 155
Nauvoo, Illinois 62354
217.453.6767

Kolbe & Kolbe Millwork Co., Inc.
1323 South 11th Avenue
Wausau, WI 54401
800.955.8666
www.kolbe-kolbe.com

Marvin Windows and Doors
P.O. Box 100
Warroad, MN 56763
888.955.8666
www.marvin.com

Velux (skylights)
800.88.VELUX
www.velux.com

WRITERS

Catherine Seiberling Pond
P.O. Box 61
Hancock, NH 03449
603.525.4235
cspond@verizon.net